MAN UPTIGHT!

MAN UPTIGHT!

By

David Augsburger

MOODY PRESS
CHICAGO

Printed in the United States of America

Contents

1

To Tell the Truth

Situation one. So you just backed your station wagon up to the dock, heaved out that borrowed fifteen-horse outboard and grunted your way down to where your scrubby little dinghy is tied. You pull the boat close, hoist the outboard, step one foot into the boat, and oh no! The old one-foot-on-the-dock-one-foot-in-the-boat gag! You're doing a split, teetering for balance, hugging your brother-in-law's motor and trying to keep the gap between boat and dock from spreading any farther.

You hang on desperately, muscles cramping, sweat in your eyes, your mind racing. What can you do? Yell for help? Nobody to hear. Drop the outboard into the boat? No, it'll go right through the bottom. You teeter—about to topple—then you let it slip. It disappears over the side.

But what else could you do? You couldn't grow wings. You couldn't walk on water. You didn't want to split. The only choice you had was to give it the heave into twenty feet of water! Now what'll you tell your touchy brother-in-law who wouldn't believe the truth anyway? Or that cynical insurance agent who won't want to pay off? Or

what will you say to your wife who didn't want you to go
fishing today anyway?

Alternatives. You sit there sweating in your battered
boat. The borrowed fifteen-horse outboard is twenty feet
down, and a not-too-sympathetic brother-in-law is going
to chew your ears right down to the sideburns.

If you could get it back, it would likely be ruined—and
if you can't? Maybe you could tell your brother-in-law it
was stolen while you stopped for bait at the marina. Chip
your little side vent window with a tire iron to prove someone broke into your car, and let his theft insurance take
care of it. Only what if he hasn't got any theft insurance?
Then you know what he'll say. "*You* lost it for me. *You*
pay."

Hey—but maybe *you* could collect for it.

You've got insurance that might cover it. (What all is
in that personal property policy? Fire, theft and storm?)
Hey, that's it. You could tell the agent the boat upset in
rough water. Storm insurance? Easy enough. Except the
motor wasn't yours. Well, have your brother-in-law write
up a phony bill of sale. Date it last month. You might even
write it for a twenty-five-horse and get paid for a bigger
motor.

But there are a few hitches. Will your brother-in-law
go along? If you ask him and he acts righteous, he's liable
to ride you about it every week. Then, there's always your
conscience, your self-respect, your sense of personal integrity. Is it worth losing all that for the cost of an outboard?

There is another alternative. Tell your insurance man
the straight scoop. There's a chance you might be covered.
He claims to be on your side; give him the dope and see
what happens. If he can't come through, tighten your belt

and pay it off with your lunch money. You could afford to lose a few pounds. ("Every cloud has a silver. . . .") Even if there are no benefits, you'll be a man you can respect. You'll not only tell the truth, you'll be true to yourself.

Situation two. So you're on the lot, trying to sell this customer a "good number one OK buy-in-a-million used car" when you get to this lemon that you got stuck with as a trade-in a year ago and can't move.

Is this the chance? You turn on the charm and spin out the sales spiel. But inside, your better sense mocks the stuff you're saying.

"Now take this car, ma'am. It's a real honey. Low mileage for its age; belonged to a little old lady. (*Who only drove it Sundays—at the drag races.*) Uses a little oil, not much of course. (*Not sitting here on the lot. But if I don't move this bomb soon it's going to get junked.*) It'd make a great second car in the family, ma'am. There are a lot of good miles left in this one. (*You can probably even get it a mile or so away from here.*)"

So that's your job. It's not that you're a dishonest man. You never lie to your wife. Your friends all trust you—but then, you never sell them cars. It's just that on the job a few things are necessary, like saying the right thing to sell. It's a speech you can use for any car—you just repeat what the customer wants to hear. It's the only way to sell. Or is it?

Alternatives. What do you do about the occupational dishonesty that business demands of you?

Accept it as one of the facts of business life? Everybody's got a few flies in the ointment. The secretary has to say, "Sorry, the boss is out and can't be reached," when she's sitting in front of him. The boss has to say, "I'd love to give you a raise, if we could only afford it, but profits are at an all-time low," just when business is peaking. And your bit is to sell those cars by saying all the noticeable nice things and smoothing over the bad.

And likely you're just as honest as the customer is when he's trading in his old one. So why think twice about it?

But how about the alternative of using the same kind of honesty at work that you use in your personal life.

It may not sell cars—for a while, at least—until people learn to trust you instead of discounting everything you say by 75 percent.

It could be a lot more relaxing. And you wouldn't need such an expert memory to remember everything you've said so that your next sales speech doesn't contradict you.

But wait. Why talk of honesty as something you do when it's advantageous or appropriate?

Isn't honesty really something that you are? Isn't it more important that a man *be* the truth rather than just tell the truth? Now if a man made that kind of choice—to be the truth whenever, wherever, whatever the situation—that could make quite a different kind of life, couldn't it?

Situation three. So your old second car began making like a percussion band last night. The motor knocks and something is pinging loosely where the valves ought to be. You're feeling sick about it all, and you want to trade it off for anything. The way that thing sounds, it isn't even worth the price of junk.

"Boy, if I could find a little old car dealer who's blind, deaf and eager to trade, maybe I could pass off this lemon," you say.

Then, an idea. Two cans of additive in the crankcase, a third in the carburetor, another in the gas, and it's running like a sewing machine—temporarily. You head for the car dealer you like least.

There you find just the car you'd like to trade for, and the dickering begins. Everything's going great until the guy says, "Say, that motor on your car sounds like something's a little loose in there. Probably nothing serious, but had any trouble with it lately?"

Here is your moment of—truth? If you hedge, he'll smell the rat and knock a couple hundred off its trade-in value—or refuse to take it at all. But if you tell him the car's A-OK, you'll hate to meet him on the street next time. But you'll have gotten rid of it.

Alternatives. You could have sent your identical twin in with the car. He could have sold it with a glowing speech and still told the truth—as far as he knew it.

Or you could sprinkle a few half-truths, like "It's never been in for an overhaul"; "She's never let me down"; or "She's worth her weight in green stamps!"

And if he senses that you're wriggling around something and gets suspicious? String him a line. Tell him anything, but get rid of that car. Sure, it *is* a bit dishonest. But could be he's getting ready to pull your leg on the one he's selling you. It's a dog-eat-dog world, isn't it? And anything goes when you're horse-trading—or car-swapping. What can you lose?

On the other hand, you could explain it all. Look the guy in the eye and tell him that your car has a few drawbacks. Might need a little mechanical work. Tell him it has a knock or two and then take what comes.

Sure he may reduce your trade-in value. He might even

refuse it. Or the shock of finding an honest customer may overwhelm him and move him to generosity.

Whatever the outcome, why make decisions of right and wrong on the basis of what you get out of it? Couldn't you choose to do the right thing simply because right is right, and opt to tell the true things because the truth is truth?

Situation four. Let's say you're working late at the office. Everyone else has punched out and you're about to call it quits yourself, when the phone rings. It's for the boss and he's out, but the caller wants to leave a message. "Tell J. B. that the deadline for bids on the new hospital has been moved up a week," the guy says. Then he asks, "Can I count on you to get the word to him?" "Of course," you say with offended dignity. You hang up, make a mental note, and head home. But by morning it's completely slipped your mind. Well, almost. A week later, the day of the deadline, it hits you. And then—dilemma!

If you own up and tell the boss immediately, he might be able to get his bid in on time. But will you ever get chewed! If he loses it, it could set the whole company back for the next three years. And what's worse, that promotion you've been angling for is hanging by a thread. This could snap it. *Why tell him, if it's going to smash my hopes for moving up* you ask yourself. He may never know who slipped up. The odds are pretty safe. Unless the guy who phoned recognized and remembers your voice. Then the phone rings. The boss himself. Calling about a few odds and ends. Then he adds, "Next week, we've got to get around to that hospital bid." Now you've got to decide. To tell or not to tell.

Alternatives. You could always try to keep mum. Why

should you have to tell everything you know? It wasn't your worry to begin with, so why not bluff your way by? Silence could save you an awful scene with the boss. If you get away with it, you'll come out smelling like a rose.

But what if you're fingered by the guy who called? Or the boss could second-guess the story and find out why he missed the deadline. How would the boss view it? Well, he'd feel that when you owed him the truth, silence is as dishonest as deliberate denial. Until now, it was an honest mistake. You goofed and forgot to write it down. So, that could happen to anyone. Straighten it out now—and you've got at least a ghost of a chance of the boss over-looking it—after he's done growling.

But try to bluff your way through, and you could be in deep trouble.

Should you make the decision on the basis of safety first? Or what pays off best?

Or can it be that honesty is a basic entrance requirement into true manhood? Isn't honesty the only way of handling the truth that matches up with the way we were created to function and make decisions? Isn't honesty the only known way to truly be at peace with yourself, your boss and your God?

As you decide. What is truth? What is tact? What is diplomacy?

Tact is important in life, if it doesn't become a tactic for handling people. Then it so easily turns to flattery, flattery to clever diplomacy, diplomacy to false exaggeration, and exaggeration to maneuvering people as things—as pieces or pawns on the chessboard of your life.

Truth is always consistent with itself. It needs no help to stand alone. But a lie is crippled. It needs a second lie for a brace, a third for a crutch. It's easy to tell one lie, but it's hard to tell only one lie.

But what is a lie? And what is lying? *Any* untrue statement? No, let's say (1) any willfully untrue statement; (2) any deliberate false representation; (3) any intentional design to mislead or deceive; (4) any attempt to withhold information another rightfully and justly deserves to know.

The key to any and all definitions of lies and lying is the intention, the motive, the attitude of heart. Any intentional deception—even though it is said in words that are true in themselves—is a lie.

No matter how true a statement may be, it can be a deliberate lie in intention. It's the motive that matters most.

It is not enough—it is never enough—to simply talk of telling the truth. A man can tell the truth and be a liar still. All he has to do is select what truths to tell, or which half-truths to combine, and with a smattering of skill and "with a little bit of luck" he can be an "honest" liar.

It is not enough to talk of telling the truth or even of telling the whole truth.

We must *be* the truth. Be true persons. Be truly human. Be true to self, be true to others and be true to God, the source of all truth.

It's one thing to say the truth—it's another to be it.

That's what makes Jesus Christ stand out.

He said, "I *am* . . . the truth" (Jn 14:6). Those nearest Him confirmed it. John writes: "God became a human being and lived among us. We saw his splendor . . . , full of grace and truth . . . for . . . love and Truth came through Jesus Christ" (Jn 1:14, 17*a*, Phillips).

And He asked us to be as true as the light, without any shadow of dishonesty in us.

> Finish, then, with lying and tell your neighbor the truth. For we are not separate units but intimately related to one another in Christ (Eph 4:25, Phillips).

What a release that is, to become a new, true person, to become the truth. And what a relief it is to be the truth. To be truly yourself before God, before others—and before yourself. No need to run and hide. No more games of hide-and-seek with your conscience. No more faking. No more playacting. No more false fronts or faces.

You're free. Free to be the truth, the whole truth and nothing but the truth—by the help of God.

2

To Cool That Temper

Scene one. So you're driving peacefully down the street, and this nut in front of you slams on his brakes just as you turn for a second look at this girl on the crosswalk. When you look back, you're almost on top of him. You hit the brakes and, well, you guessed it, his trunk looks like an elephant tramped it, and the steam's rolling up from your busted radiator. "You *idiot!*" the guy yells, charging out of his Camaro. "What's the big idea? Get outa that bucket of bolts and I'll do an accordion job on your nose."

"Now calm down," you say, "it's just a little bump. An accident's an accident. It can all be fixed."

"Fixed, nothin'!" the guy snarls, "You're the one that needs fixin' and I aim to do the honors—free of charge, too."

A crowd is gathering on the sidewalk, no cop in sight, and the stuff that the guy is saying about your mother isn't any too nice. What can you do? How do you face an angry man?

Alternatives. Shall you snap back with a bit of your own

16

anger, eat humble pie, give him a bit of scalding silence, stick out your jaw and take the punch, or run?

The first reaction most of us feel is "Don't take all that lip! Give him a little of your own."

Advantages? Well, you show the guy what's what. You get a second or two of release from some of your own tensions. But when you're obviously in the wrong, it's not going to ease the situation much to lose your head. In fact, facing an angry man with anger is adding fuel to his fire.

Maybe you should try the alternative of fast action. He's got his dukes up to take a poke at you? Call his bluff, make like it's a Middle East crisis and punch him while he's still threatening. Advantages? I can't think of any. Disadvantages? You bet. The first blow is a confession of weakness higher up, of failure to think, and of a shortage of self-control.

What's the next alternative? Well, you can eat humble pie and accept full blame with a complete apology. Your insurance man will like that even less than your having the wreck in the first place.

But what about silence? So the guy's lost his cool—just stand there and let him vent his spleen. There's nothing much more scalding than pure silence. And when he runs out of steam power—will he feel cheap. Disadvantages? One. 'Tain't easy.

But there's one other alternative. Be understanding. Try to feel what the other guy's going through. So he's just driving his new Camaro home for the first time. And at the first traffic light—you. If you can feel just a touch of his frustration, you might be able to say the right thing. Ever hear the old proverb "A soft answer turns away wrath, but a harsh word stirs up anger" (Pr 15:1, RSV)?

But how do you get just the right answer?

It helps to have a bit of extra strength inside you. The strength that comes from loving God and loving your neighbor as yourself.

Scene two. So you've just come out of the office, heading for the elevator, when you see the guy stepping on who's getting the big promotion. That promotion was your piece of cake, and he stole it! You're not about to ride down with him tonight, so you stop, fumble in your pocket, faking like you forgot something, and head back into the office.

No wonder you hate his guts. He got his degree from Harvard; you worked yours out at city college night school. He married the second vice-president's daughter and, what's more, she was a college beauty queen. But what really bugs you is that he overheard you explaining your pet idea for promoting the Jones' account; he took it to the boss; he stole credit for it; and it's putting him over the top.

So he's getting your promotion—and you? You hate him like the devil.

You turn to leave and as you pass his office, you see it. His whole presentation is all laid out for tomorrow's big meeting. There it is, your idea. He's fleshed it out and tomorrow, the final killing. You look both ways, step into the office, scoop up the papers, stuff them into your brief-case and before you know what you've done, you're in the hall pushing the elevator "down" button. Then, a few words from your conscience. "So you sabotage him and he turns up empty-handed tomorrow. What good will that do you? So you've got a mighty big grudge against him, what's it going to help to feed it?" Just then the elevator arrives. "Going down?" asks the operator. Then you've got to decide.

Alternatives. So what do you do when you've the chance of a lifetime to get even with the one man who's been tramping all over you?

The guy's really got it coming. He's stolen your promotion by plagiarizing your ideas. Now you've got your chance. If you burn the presentation you just lifted from his office, it's your idea going up in smoke (with a bit of his work attached).

So why not a bit of sweet revenge? Everything inside you insists, "He fouled me, let him hurt a little!" If you get even, your sense of justice will have been squared—maybe. Then too, you'll be contributing to the education of a scrambling climber who needs it—badly. You'll do him the favor of trimming him down to size. And, most needed of all, you'll vent your hostility and drain off a bit of anger.

But revenge is powerless to solve the real problem or to salve your real hurt. You can't get repayment for the wrong he has done to you. Repayment is impossible. Nor can you take it out of his hide in revenge, because: (1) it usually boomerangs somehow; (2) it won't—and can't—restore anything you've lost; (3) it is not an effective or pleasant release of your anger; instead it turns it into a long slow burn of hostility and hatred; (4) it only adds anxiety and regrets to the burden of anger, making your feelings even worse; (5) in the end, revenge damages your character and integrity, and breeds even deeper frustration and depression.

The man who takes revenge is as foolish as the guy who puts the barrel of a gun against his chest and squeezes off a shot, hoping to hurt his enemy with the kick of its recoil.

The alternative? Forgive him. It's the only way that can begin to make things right, to begin healing over a nasty situation—emotionally, mentally and spiritually. And that's the only real release for the frustration you feel.

Yes, of course it's one of the hardest things any man ever does. Forgiving a thing like this demands so much of you in understanding and in soaking up the other guy's punches without punching back.

Is that why so few ever attempt it? And even fewer achieve it? But when you know what it's like to be forgiven—to be forgiven by God the way He showed us in Jesus Christ—then you know you've got the resources to forgive somebody else.

Scene three. The first time you met the man, you could tell that he was something different. He was—well, take the first day he showed up at work, when old Jonesy, the shop's laziest clown, says to him, "Hey, you forgot to clean up under the benches," shoving his dirty work onto the new guy. "Sorry," the fellow says, "didn't see you needed help. Be glad to!" And he grabs the broom and has it all swept up before Jonesy gets over everybody's laughs.

And a couple weeks later, when the cops picked up Smitty back in the paint shop (they got him for forging checks), this new guy knocks off work, with a cut in pay, to go to court with him. "He needed a friend," he says. "The hot spot in court's the loneliest place on earth."

But what really set you wondering happened today when Bill took a poke at him (he'd bumped Bill's coffee thermos off the bench—accidentally). He takes the punch, then says, "Bill, anybody ever give you a second crack—at his other cheek? Here." Did Bill hit him? Huh-uh. Bill looked like you'd run over him with a truck.

That's what set you thinking. Why'd the guy do that? Why would anybody deliberately ask for another punch? What would you do if a guy took a wild poke at you?

Alternatives. So what do you do when the other fellow's pushing, taking unfair advantage, or even has his fist under your nose?

The first thing that comes to mind, especially if he's smaller, is to give him a bit of his own medicine. You've got to stand up to the guy or he'll walk all over you. Bust his lip and break this thing off for good.

Only—if you hit him back, likely it wouldn't stop with trading just one set of lumps, unless that's a pretty powerful Sunday punch you're going to uncork.

Violence in return usually breeds more violence.

You could just turn and walk off. That leaves the guy hanging unjustified for what he's done. But once you hit him back, he'll feel he was in the right. Ignoring him may hit harder than your fist.

Or if you want to really clobber him—with a weapon that leaves him defenseless and embarrassed—you could try nonviolence. Turn the other cheek and ask him if he needs a second crack at you. It shows him you're controlling your anger, you're still accepting him in spite of what he's done, and that you're unwilling to stoop to his level of violence as a way of solving any problem.

But of course you're running the risk of getting punched again. He may just take you up on it and you'll find yourself hearing the birdies tweet-tweet in some dreamland meadow.

But then, if you once get the courage to try turning the other cheek, you probably won't choose that way just because it's the safest. You may choose it because it's the only way to do something about helping the other guy get over his hair-trigger temper. Maybe you could choose it because it's the way of Christ?

As you decide. I have some. You have some. We all have them. Impossible people.

What makes people impossible?

Each of us can quickly compile our own list. Obvious pride often comes first; then boasting; insisting on one's own way; superior, condescending actions; open anger and malice; conspicuous consumption of wealth; chronic hyper-critical attitudes; a holier-than-thou spirit; a gossip gourmet—the list is endless.

But wait, you have friends—dear friends—who are just as guilty of any or many of these traits as are some of the people you like least. You can overlook it in your own set, forgive it in your friends. Why not in those people you consider hopeless and hapless?

Could it be that the problem is not all in the other person? That part—a sizable part—perhaps a major part—is our problem, not theirs?

Can it be that what makes people impossible is not as much their fault as it is ours? Or is that an overstatement? Would you believe it's fifty-fifty?

Whatever the fraction on who's causing the friction, one thing is clear. If we're going to have any success on living with impossible people, it will have to come by the change we make in our own selves first.

We will need to deal with our problems before we qualify to help the other person with his.

But how do we go about identifying what makes us irritable and angry toward others?

Often the best yardstick is to ask, "What irritates me most in the other guy?" Then use it as a mirror. So often we hate in others what we recognize but won't admit is present in our own lives.

Check those situations for size. Do they come near fitting?

Have you ever had to face up to the fact that you can't get what you want, or must lose what you had, so (1) you criticize those who may have stood in the way? or (2) you blame your own mismanagement on others who seem to be prospering? or (3) you dislike those who have what you don't and hold it against them for getting it and enjoying it in front of you? or (4) you begrudge those who succeed in your field, and show it by "helping to keep them humble," by chipping away at their success with criticism or occasional rumors that may slow down their progress?

Certainly you've had most of these things done to you by some of the impossible people around you. Can you see any of them in yourself?

Are there any clues to living with difficult personalities?

1. Our own suspicions of others might be replaced with trust.

2. Our own jealousies of others could be redirected into concern.

3. Our own selfishness should bend to broaden into love of others.

4. Our own fears can be softened by faith in God and man.

5. Our own pride and prejudice must be converted into warm understanding of self and of others.

Then we would begin living. Living as peacemakers. Living as the kind of healing persons who buffer the high acidity common among people who just can't stomach each other.

The lubrication of love for others can reduce friction remarkably. A strange change happens when you recognize that the impossible people around you are hungry for acceptance, love and trust. Show me a cold fish who turns you off, and I'll show you a person resorting to desperate means to save and protect what little security, safety and emotional warmth he has and hungry for more of the same.

Apply the gentle lubrication of love to your relationships with others, and you will be astounded at what a change it will work in you and them.

Live as though *live* and *love* were one and the same. Let "love" become your way of life and what a change will follow.

"But wait," you may say, "that's all well and fine with irritating people, with frustrating people, but not with the impossible ones. Them I can't love!"

Correction! Them you can't like. Not yet. But you can love them. Love? Yes. Christian love is the decision of your will to act in a concerned, responsible way toward another whether you like him or not. Love is not something you feel; it's something you do. Love is not an emotion that just comes naturally; it's an action that comes from an inner decision to follow Jesus Christ's way of helpful, self-forgetful, purposeful compassion.

It begins in the will. When I will to do Christ's will. When it is demonstrated in action, then it begins to penetrate and slowly effect a change in your feelings toward others. Yes, you will discover what it is to like the unlikable, to love the unlovely, the unloving, even the unlovable.

That is why Christ unhesitatingly commanded that we love. It is His new commandment. You cannot command the heart to love, but the will? Yes. The command to love is a call to men of character to commit themselves to a life of loving acceptance, understanding and service to their fellowmen. Impossible or not.

3

What's a Marriage For?

Scene one. So you just switched on the TV and sat down in your favorite chair to let your supper settle. That warm afterdinner glow is just getting through to you. You're an old married man now—four weeks of bliss. Honeymoon, travel, vacation, moving, furnishing the apartment—all that is history now! You've worked like a dog getting everything straight. Now you can relax.

Then it comes. The voice from the kitchen. "John, dear." "Yes." "Will you come run the garbage out?" "You're kidding?" you reply, keeping your voice light. "It's on the table," she says. "That bundle in the newspaper."

"Thanks all the same, but I'm comfortable," you say with a bit of firmness, hoping she'll catch the hint. After all, anyone knows that carrying out the gook is woman's work. Your dad wouldn't have touched it, so why should you?

Then she appears at the door. "Please, John," she says, "I've got the dishes to do, then clean up out here—It'll only take you a minute."

This is the moment to make your position clear. "Let's

get it straight from the start," you say. "Garbage is hardly my responsibility. I'll do anything else around the house before I'll start on that."

Suddenly your eyes lock in conflict. And you begin to wonder if you haven't pushed this a little far. After all, she's worked hard to please you. Then she turns and disappears into the kitchen. The feeling of her silent anger begins to gnaw at you. A small decision can affect your life for a long time. How do you choose?

Alternatives. Pretty small stuff, deciding to help or not to help your wife with kitchen chores, or to carry or not to carry out the garbage. But wait—there may be quite a conflict concealed in that simple little tangle.

Let's say you weaken, get up and carry out the scraps. The job's nothing; it's the precedent you're setting. Doing woman's work. And that's not your role. You're hardly being a man if you start playing maid. So it fights with your feelings about manhood. Should you bend and bow to her wishes? Become Mr. Milquetoast?

So she expects you to be like her dad, to do things like he did. That's the trouble. Or is it your image and expectations of her that are on trial? You're expecting her to be a wife that does all the things your mother did, and she's been planning on something else.

If you give in and cart out the carrot tops, your ideas of marriage will have to bend a bit. If you don't help, she'll have to learn to take it and like it. Either way, there's bound to be a bit of adjusting to be done.

Does that mean you will say, "Me man—you woman. Me sit in chair with paper, you wash dish and lug out gook"? Or will you give in and run that mission to the garbage can?

Why the fuss over who does odd jobs around the kitchen, the house, or the yard? Because your life together— whether you've been married four days or forty years—is determined a great deal by how you view your role as man or woman. And there's a lot more to it than learning to handle a toothpaste tube alike—if you're a squeezer and she's a roller.

The real adjustment is in the fundamental decision to "be the right mate," rather than trying to remake the other into "just the right mate." If you're in this marriage routine for basically what you get out of it, stay put in your chair. But if you're in it to build a wholesome homelife of happiness for both of you, then think again about doing your part, whatever it may be.

Scene two. You come home bushed, bone-tired from a rough, tough day, and you hear the noise in the house from clear out at the drive. You open the door cautiously. Sure enough, everything in the house is upside down, the kids are having a rainy-day riot and your wife is in the kitchen, nerves frayed to a hair.

"Go in there and settle those kids for me," she says.

"Sorry," you say, heading for your den. "You let them get out of hand, you can cool them off. After all, they're your kids."

"Whattaya mean, 'they're my kids'?" she snaps. "You were involved a bit too, or don't you remember?"

"Now look," you say, "I fight the world for a paycheck— that's my bit. You bring up the kids—that's a woman's bit. Isn't that fair enough?"

She's speechless as you drop all your things on the desk in the den. Then, as you grab the door to shut out the roar from the living room, she gets in the usual last word, with a rather pointed remark. "Since when did you resign from being a father?" she asks.

You start to snort a reply, but the words don't come. She's gotten through to you—right in there where you live. "Of course I'm being a father," you mutter, "but I'm not going to be a mother too." You switch on the TV and settle into an armchair. Inside you've squelched the argument her words had almost stirred up. Then there's this tremendous crash in the living room. That does it with you. You're out of the den with blood in your eye.

In the hallway, you collide with your wife. "Oh," she says, "you're going to get involved after all, now that someone needs to be spanked."

"Oh, never mind," you say, swinging back toward the den, but she cuts you off. "Please, dear," she says, "can't you give me a hand with the kids till dinner's ready? You can't cool them off just with threats. Take them outside to pitch ball or— Well, you always think of something."

Yeah, sure you do, but not after a rough day like today. Is it too much for a man to expect a little peace and quiet at home? So what's a father to do? Come home and do all his wife's work too? Or is raising the kids really wife's work?

Alternatives. When your wife points out how little you're helping in raising the kids and accuses you of bowing out from being a father, what do you do?

You could tell her to get her marbles straight and quit trying to unload her job on you at the end of the day. If she'd been keeping them busy all day like you're paying her to—well, like she's supposed to—things wouldn't come to this. After all, having kids, raising kids, feeding kids, clothing kids, disciplining kids, teaching kids, that's her job, right? Your part? Well, you're needed to get her started and to provide the cash for house and spouse. But beyond that? It's her sweat! Let her worry.

You could tell her that, but not right now. Right now she better get help of some kind from you or you're going to be in hot water in a few minutes—followed by a cold shoulder all week. But as you help, you can rub it in that she's taking your only few minutes of peace and quiet after all that work you've suffered through for her paycheck.

Or you could listen to her. Maybe she has a point? Could be a father has a few responsibilities at home? If you hear her out, it will at least help drain a little of her anger. And you might even enjoy the kids in spite of the noise.

Maybe you do owe her a little more cooperative help. Perhaps raising kids was meant to be a fifty-fifty proposition; if so, you'll have to start putting in a little more time.

If you're going to be the dad a real family needs to build healthy, stable kids, you'll need to make a few changes, give a little more effort and get a lot more involved.

And isn't that part of the design for marriage—and for fathers—that God intended?

Scene three. You worked twenty minutes late at the office, stopped for an item or two at the drugstore and got held up by the line at the cash register. Then, to top it off, a traffic snarl tied you up on the freeway. You're an hour late getting home.

As you step in the door, the hostility hits you like high humidity; the anger's hanging heavy in the air. You drop your coat over a chair and head to the kitchen. She's working at the counter. "Hi," you say, tossing your cheery voice at her back. "I'm home from the wars, or is it the heartless

jungles of labor?" No answer. She turns slowly. Long
smoldering irritation lies on her lids. "You could have
called," she says icily, and with finality. Then she turns
back to her work of salvaging an overdone, overcooked
supper. You try to think of an appropriate way of justifying yourself, but you just don't have the energy or the will
to start. Why try to explain the last-minute job that took
twice as long as expected, or the rush in the store or the
impossible traffic. You let the silence mount and slowly
her anger begins to infect you, too. Why must she fly into
such a tizzy when things beyond your control interfere?

Now what shall you do? Eat humble pie for appetizer?
Suffer through a silent supper, a long, still evening? And
maybe a cold night? Or should you try to force her to talk
it out?

Alternatives. How do you respond to your wife's silent
anger that's simmering away out there in the kitchen
where she's stewing?

You can let her anger get into your blood and then vent
it all right back on her. Give her the old look-how-nice-
you've-got-it-loafing-here-at-home-all-day-while-I'm-work-
ing-my-fingers-to-the-bone line. Admittedly that's not the
"most likely to succeed" angle. And you may wind up with
egg on your face (soup and spuds too). So venting your
rising hostility is out. What then?

Give her her own silence in return? Nothing will get
through to her better—all the way through her skin. Yet
you know that the longer these things fester, the harder
they are to heal.

You could try to force her to talk about it. Will she welcome that? Well, that may all depend on the time of day,
the time of the month or the timing you use. If you start

off with a good self-justification, you'll go over like vinegar-flavored candy. Or you could hash over the last six fights you had over your erratic schedule or unexplained absences. But will you gain anything by it?

Or perhaps you should go one step deeper. Try a bit of frank, undefensive discussion with her on what really lies behind these angry spells. Stewing on anger is not only treacherous for a marriage, it's poison to your personality and to your personal mental health. Plus, it can cause all sorts of hangups for the kids.

Why not talk it out—honestly. And if that doesn't seem to work—why not open it up together with a counselor. After all, if it were your car that was breaking down, you'd take it to an expert. If your marriage is smoldering slowly, why not care enough to get help? Your minister or a respected counselor can do a lot more for your happiness than you'd imagine.

And then too, opening up the problems that rankle you can be a great step toward freeing your marriage so that it can start becoming the great thing it was designed to be. With trust, respect, loyalty and all those other things that make up love—as the Creator intended us to love.

As you decide. Any marriage between humans has problems because humans are problems. Every marriage is infected with self-centeredness from both sides. Misunderstanding is unavoidable, tension unpreventable, anger inescapable, conflict inevitable.

But conflict, not combat. If tensions are allowed to separate you, alienate you and frustrate you with resentments, they will be destructive. When they should be constructive! The differences between man and woman were designed, by the Designer, to be complementary. We were created uniquely male and female yet incomplete in ourselves, each in need of a permanent union to another to discover the complete fulfillment of personhood. The differences of emotional response, role and responsibility which often give birth to conflict are meant to be the central spring of creativity.

Conflict can be creative. It can be used creatively to make better, richer, more complete persons of both man and woman.

How we face, accept and understand conflict makes the crucial difference. Instead of such difficulty causing a marriage breakdown, it can be the means to a breakthrough to new intimacy and understanding.

If! If we are willing to understand, to learn, to practice the art of making our conflicts creative, not catastrophic. The two options—to create or to destroy—are always open before us.

Erich Fromm, the noted psychoanalyst, has written, "The man who cannot create wants to destroy."

And it happens habitually in marriage, where the competition of two contrasting persons and personalities produces conflicts which can be disastrous. Unless, creatively, we let conflict be constructive. Where do we begin?

By realizing that love is not the absence of conflicts, nor is conflict any indication that love is absent.

By recognizing "most husband-wife conflict comes out indirectly over substitute issues and eventuates in stalemate because the central differences do not come into the open," as Gibson Winter incisively comments.*

*Gibson Winter, *Love and Conflict: New Patterns in Family Life* (Garden City, N. Y.: Doubleday, 1958), p. 115.

By realizing that most of what we call "conflicts" in marriage are only symptoms, minor superficial disagreements which are actually a cover for the real conflict beneath.

By smiling at these surface conflicts, when you see them for what they are, and refusing to stalemate over these pointless frictions that clutter daily relationships.

By recognizing that the real conflicts which we must deal with eventually are the difficulties and differences that we hide and hesitate to face, since they are threatening to our own comfort and well-being.

By seeking to understand the real issues of difference between the two of you, and deal honestly with them in both conversation and action.

By risking deeper conflict in opening up the actual differences, not for argument or combat, but for a venture into intimacy. (Our longing for intimacy with another can lead us to substitute a false togetherness by avoiding all threatening issues, tiptoeing around each other like ballet dancers walking on eggs.)

By truly accepting your marriage partner with his or her differences, identifying yourselves together in the face of your difficulties and asking, "How can we make these dilemmas bring us together rather than wedge us apart?"

How do we use conflict creatively?

By facing, understanding, accepting and resolving our differences constructively.

But where do we find the strength for such a life style, for such a fundamental commitment to being creative right at the point where we naturally and inevitably tend to be destructive?

Having looked at the blueprint for complementary lives

in creative marriage, let's look at the design for our own selves. The original design by our Maker.

We were meant to discover lives of creative beauty, of constructive worth. We who are expressions of the Creator's creativity were created to be co-workers in His own creativity, turning the tragedies of this world into triumphs.

As the Bible describes our role in expressing God's creativity in life:

> God, who is rich in mercy,
> Because of His great love for us,
> Gave us the gift of life
> Together with Christ.
> Thus He shows for all time
> His great generosity, grace and kindness
> Expressed toward us in Christ Jesus.
> What we are, we owe
> To the touch of His creativity,
> For we are His workmanship,
> His poems, His creative expressions,
> Created anew in Christ Jesus
> To lives of goodness and good deeds
> Which God planned before
> For us to do (Eph 2:4-5, 7, 10, author's paraphrase)

Now, how does this emerge in life? In difficulty, in conflict?

It appears as an eagerness to face the hardships of life and see how they can be resolved in new meaning and strength.

Listen again to the Bible's advice:

> When all kinds of trials and temptations crowd into your lives, my brothers, don't resent them as intruders, but welcome them as friends! Realize that they come to

test your faith and to produce in you the quality of endurance. But let the process go on until that endurance
is fully developed, and you will find you have become
men of mature character with the right sort of independ-
ence. And if, in the process, any of you does not know
how to meet any particular problem he has only to ask
God—who gives generously to all men without making
them feel foolish or guilty—and he may be quite sure that
the necessary wisdom will be given him (Ja 1:2-5, Phillips).

But does it work in life? Does it work! Yes, yes, it does.

Those who commit themselves to love husband or wife
both because of what they are and in spite of what they
aren't discover the first step toward the spring of daily
creativity—unconditional love. Isn't that what a marriage
pledge really is anyway?

And those who commit themselves to unconditional
fidelity, in body, mind and spirit, won't let differences
create distance; they turn them into new levels of understanding.

And those who share a common loyalty, an absolute
allegiance to Jesus Christ, discover not only the union of
common faith, but the communion of sharing in a common
strength to love, to forgive and to be forgiven. This is possible because they share common experiences of inner
change and transformation through the Holy Spirit which
gives an uncommon meaning in life.

All this through the creative Spirit of Christ. The Holy
Spirit, the Bible says, brought the entire creation out of a
universe of chaos.

The Holy Spirit brings a new creation into being in any
man's life when and if he responds in faith.

And the Holy Spirit can provide the creative strength to make life's understandings and misunderstandings sparkle with constructive growth, if we follow Christ in all of life.

Can your life be an expression of His creativity?

4

On Using Others

Scene one. You're walking down the street, enjoying your lunch break, feeling the spring breeze on your face, and pursuing your favorite spectator sport—girl watching. Just then this dream comes around the corner. Your eyes eagerly drink in the rich gold of her hair, the creamy complexion, the beauty in the way she moves.

Inside your mind, the secret life of Walter Mitty grinds away. "Hi," you say, in your best imaginary voice, your most dashing smile in place. "Haven't we met?"

"Not in my lifetime," she replies, but the lift of her eyebrow excuses your impertinence.

"Now that we just did," you say with a twinkle, "let's make the most of it."

She looks at you icily for a moment, a hint of anger appears, and then (as is always the case in your dreams), she melts. "Certainly no harm in that," she says, with a fluttered eyelid.

"I wouldn't go so far as to say that," you reply, with your famous charm.

Then you're strolling, arms brushing, making conversation. Then the scene in your cinema-of-the-mind does a fade; and you're sitting with her by the ocean, the moon is highlighting her hair with gold, and her head is gentle on your shoulder.

Now she's past you, swinging down the sidewalk. You snap back from your dream, turn for the last walk-away view, and then "eyes-front" for the next leading lady to star in your own continuing drama of "My Imaginary Life and Loves."

And then you wonder. *Why do I run on and on like this, secretly, mentally using those I meet? What's the matter with me? Or does every man do it, like me?*

Alternatives. So what about this sport of girl watching? Don't most men do it a bit more than they admit? What can compete? So the boys watch the girls and the girls watch the boys. Nice arrangement. Except for what may happen in the bedroom of your mind. Not always so nice. But what are the alternatives?

Obviously, the most natural thing is to conceal it and enjoy it. Do it with taste—so her eyes don't catch you exploring. Do it with a touch of disinterest on your face—so she won't guess what's going on behind your eyes. Do it with class on the exterior—but inside, no holds barred, nothing taboo. The advantages are obvious. There are mental playmates everywhere you look, mental affairs available any time you want to dream, and mental escapades just as exciting as you are creative.

On the negative side, there are a few considerations: (1) the man whose thoughts feature one escapade after another sees a beautiful woman not as a person to be appreciated and respected but as a body to be exploited; (2) it slowly brings on the playboy attitude that views

women as the grandest of all consumer goods, to be used
and discarded like old Kleenex; (3) what a man does and
is on the inside, he tends to become on the outside; (4) no
one really hides his thoughts, unless he's blind: your eyes
give you away time after time.

A second alternative would be to admire that beautiful
girl, but do it with genuine respect. Here's a checklist that
may help find the way through: (1) admire beauty in all
its loveliness, but do it only with sincerity and respect;
(2) view others not as sex symbols or appealing bodies
but as persons, as people made in the image of God; (3)
refuse to use them like things, because it would make each
of us less than human; (4) pledge to be in thought what
you want to be and become in action.

Scene two. You're driving home from that great late
date. It's long after midnight, but you've forgotten the
time. You're just driving. And thinking. You almost made
it tonight, and just when you thought she was going with
you to the motel room, suddenly you didn't want her to.
You hoped she'd say no. She saw it in your eyes, felt the
hesitancy in your voice, and gave you an excuse. You remember the relief you felt as you drove away from the
motel; you recall the apology you stammered out. How
could you explain it? Explain the feelings that tumbled
around inside you earlier as you pulled up by the motel
office and said, "They have a lovely restaurant here, and
a room comes with it. Shall we?" As you saw in her eyes
the slow and almost sad yes coming, you turned away.
The moments of her silence ticked tensely by until she
said, "Let's not." And then, the relief of laughter. Embarrassed, brittle laughter that told more than you wanted
it to.

What will you say to her next time? Shall you explain? Tell her that somehow love seems more sensitive, more fragile, more precious than you thought; and if you rushed ahead, it might be crushed and things would change between you?

Or should you forget those cautious moments? There's always tomorrow night, and you could try again, and again. But is that what you want?

You're not sure. If you marry, wouldn't it be better to start off clean? With no unpleasant memories? But how do you decide?

Alternatives. If you do go ahead—provided she's willing —yes, you will get to know her in a new way. But the disadvantages?

You love the girl, and somehow that love makes you want to respect her, not to use her in any way. And that respect makes you want whatever will make her happiest, whatever will build her self-respect, help her to the long-term adjustments you'll both need to make for a happy marriage. You can't—and don't—expect too many of those from premarital sex.

Remember, she has a lot more hesitancy about discarding her virginity than you do; so if either of you is going to suffer psychological damage, it would likely be she. Perhaps that's why you hate to push this. If you went to bed, and the guilt of it all, or the lack of fulfillment that she might experience, would break down trust and build a wall between you, what then?

Maybe you should apologize for the arm-twisting and tell her you intend to respect her integrity? Tell her you love her too much to do anything that might hurt her and

your love and life together? Can you imagine what that
could do for both of you?

You'll have shown her real maturity, integrity, responsibility, respect, and—most of all—love. What's more, you'll
be far more free. You'll be free to face each other without
regrets, free to understand each other in a growing intimacy of relationship without the inhibitions premarital sex
produces with all its furtiveness and forced situations. And
you'll be free to give yourselves to each other completely
in that state of complete self-giving called marriage.

Scene three. It's Monday morning, 7:30 A.M. Your feet
hit the floor, your body's up, but your head is fogged with
sleep. "Four hours of sleep just aren't enough," you tell
yourself, seeing your bloodshot eyes in the mirror. "Now
why'd I have to stay out so late again?"

Then you remember. Remember getting back to her
apartment at midnight, inviting yourself up for coffee so
you'd stay awake driving home—or what was the excuse
you used? And one thing led to another, and another, until there wasn't any other left. Well, sweet memories! Except—something about it is hurting now. Was it what she
said as you were leaving the apartment? She'd been so
quiet as you were brushing off your clothes, so you absent-
ly, teasingly said, "Well, I'll see you tomorrow night, same
time, same station." And she snapped, "Oh, no you won't,
never again. You fooled me once. I don't like being used."

Did the others feel like that too?

To you, it's all been big fun. Candy for the asking—or
pressuring and persuading.

"Oh, forget it," you tell yourself. "So she had a few sour
grapes, so what?"

But your conscience won't let you off that easily. *Forget*

it, huh? Why didn't you? You tried, but you can't, can you? The truth cut a little deep.

"OK," you retort, "so it's the truth for her, but the truth about me is, I'm a man who needs a lot—"

No, the truth is you're just taking advantage of any girl you can get.

So what do you do with a conscience like that? Avoid it and keep on moving from girl to girl? Ignore these second thoughts the morning after?

Or change your slick routine to suit your conscience?

Alternatives. What about that argument with your conscience? Should you do something about that bone your conscience is forever picking with you? Or try to shut it off?

But how do you turn off an irritating conscience? Ignore it? Hardly. Try to put it out of commission? Can't. Actually, 20 percent of it is the scale of right and wrong, standard equipment built into you by your Maker; 30 percent is worry about getting caught; and the other 50 percent is good old-fashioned common sense and values. You can't afford to turn that off!

If you go on with your game, you have to learn to live with those questioning thoughts the morning after, until they finally give up.

Of course, if living peaceably with yourself rates on your scale of values, consider the alternate way of life.

Like getting to know, understand, and love your female friends with true personal respect. Premarital sex has a way of freezing relations, frustrating genuine acceptance of each other, and thwarting open communication.

Somehow sex before the honest commitment called marriage seems too much like using the other person. Can you be satisfied to go on manipulating others for the temporary release it gives, when it creates more conflict within you than it solves?

Or there's always the alternative of trying to reeducate what's left of your conscience, readjust the old value system that makes you less than comfortable, and rationalize the objections you recognize.

Or, if personal integrity holds greater value for you; if respecting others as you want to be respected matters to you; if caring honestly about others as much as you care about yourself is one of your goals, then you may choose to take seriously the original design God had in mind when He blueprinted us to be genuine, concerned, and responsible in our relationships to others.

As you decide. When you think on dreams of being the great lover, examine what Jesus Christ said:

> "You have heard that it was said to the people in the old days, '*Thou shalt not commit adultery.*' But I say to you that every man who looks at a woman lustfully has already committed adultery with her—in his heart.
>
> "Yes, if your right eye leads you astray pluck it out and throw it away; it is better for you to lose one of your members than that your whole body should be thrown onto the rubbish heap" (Mt 5:27-29, Phillips).

Was Christ recommending blindness? No, He was recommending a life of dignity, purity, and integrity. And He valued such a life so highly that He called men to discard the things that lead to temptation. He insisted that anything that seduces us to sin be mercilessly cut out of our lives. That is the meaning of His graphic illustration of blinding yourself rather than living enslaved to lustful eyes.

What was Christ forbidding? Look closely. Don't misunderstand Him. It is deliberate, lustful looking that He challenges. The man who looks at a woman with the intention of lusting after her body is an adulterer.

But how can you avoid it? If you assume that this means any look is forbidden, any awareness of another's physical attractiveness is prohibited, any feeling of appreciation or admiration is taboo, then you might as well give up. You'll never make it. Neither will your friends.

But if you accept exactly what Christ said, a new perspective emerges. He did not question admiration of others, appreciation of beauty, or attention shown out of sincere respect.

It is right to recognize another's beauty or loveliness. It is wrong to mentally explore or exploit that beauty for selfish or sensual gratification.

And about personal chastity—consider what the Bible points out in its incisive analysis of what we are and what we are meant to be.

> God's plan is to make you holy, and that entails first of all a clean cut with sexual immorality. Every one of you should learn to control his body, keeping it pure and treating it with respect, and never regarding it as an instrument for self-gratification, as do pagans with no knowledge of God. You cannot break this rule without in some way cheating your fellow men. It is not for nothing that the Spirit God gives us is called the *Holy* Spirit (1 Th 4:3-6, 8*b*, Phillips).

> Avoid sexual looseness like the plague! Every other sin that a man commits is done outside his own body, but

this is an offense against his own body. Have you forgotten that your body is the temple of the Holy Spirit, who lives in you, and is God's gift to you, and that you are not the owner of your own body? You have been bought, and at what a price! Therefore bring glory to God in your body (1 Co 6:18-20, Phillips).

Think deeply on this; think long before acting. Consider all the issues involved in your decisions of sexuality.

Chastity is a freedom, not a restriction. It results in greater liberty, not inhibition. The standards of the Bible are given to protect your personal freedom, to enable you to become a confident, secure, regret-free, and maturing adult. Chastity provides the freedom to give yourself truly in a totally fulfilling way in the responsible relationship of unconditionally loving allegiance called marriage.

Chastity is maturity, because it respects one's own personality and personhood, and is responsible to the self-esteem and happiness of the other. Chastity is integrity—morally, physically, emotionally, and spiritually.

Consider it carefully, because it's your choice.

5

It's Work, Work, Work!

Scene one. So you're phoning your wife from the office to tell her you'll be working late again.

"Hello, dear? Why, honey, I'll have to work late again tonight. . . . Yeah. . . . I'll grab a sandwich at the drugstore downstairs. . . . Sure. . . I'll be right here. You can call me any time up till 8:30, then I'll be home by 9:00. . . . What? . . .*What?* Well, thank you very much!"

You look at the phone. It's hung up, but you still hear her talking. Those last words—did you hear her right? She said, "You might as well stay at the office all the time. Even when you are home, your mind's still doing overtime, so, good-bye."

Now why'd she have to say that? What's bugging her? Does she think you might not be working? Maybe fooling around with another woman? No, how could that be? Your job hardly gives you time for one woman; you couldn't have a second.

Well, you'll have to talk it out with her when you have time.

When you have time? Time for your wife, your kids, your family life? Say, if you keep on working like this, when will you have time for anything but getting ahead in your business?

The phone again. It's the boss himself. "Say, about that account for tomorrow," he says. "Now, I'm counting on you to stick with it tonight."

Then you feel like telling him. Telling him you'll be knocking off at quitting time tonight and every night when it's not an emergency. Tell him you happen to have a family at home. You wait for a pause in his spiel, trying to decide whether to play along as usual or to put your foot down.

How will you decide about that work schedule that's making a business widow of your wife?

Alternatives. Shall you tell the boss to count you out for tonight? Tell him you're going home tonight to get re-acquainted with your wife and kids? Remind him of all the overtime, of all the extra work you've been putting in for the old organization? Ask if you can't have a few moments for your marriage, too?

Or, maybe you see no way except to play along with the business establishment and do what needs to be done. And your wife?

You can suggest that she adjust to your putting in all the overtime that's asked of you. After all, she's happy enough for the extra cash it brings in. And then, it's your profession. It's got to come first. If you're willing to make the sacrifices necessary for achieving success, she should be able to put up with a few inconveniences. She can learn to like it.

But then, you may have to admit, she's right. Your work

has become your life. Your family gets a slim slice from what's left.

But wait. There is another alternative. Why can't a man block out time for his wife and children first? The other responsibilities—work, recreation, and the odd jobs you get stuck with—can take care of themselves.

You could base your schedule on your real scale of priorities. That would protect you from sacrificing the most valuable just to succeed in the less. And in the first place, weren't marriage and parenthood intended to be near the top on any man's list of values? Didn't the original Designer—God—blueprint our lives to find fulfillment truly in each other, not in things or wealth? And didn't He show us—in Jesus Christ—what it's like to put persons first, not things first.

Scene two. So you're lying there stark awake worrying. Not about one thing in particular, but about everything in general. Like all those bills you found in the stack of mail tonight. And like the tiff you had with your wife afterward, when she wasn't the one who made most of them anyway. Oh, except the medicine from the drugstore. But it was the kids who caught the flu and complications.

Why'd you blame her?

Or the food bills; but you can't kick on them. You're the guy who'd been griping about the steady diet of hamburger.

"What's the matter," you had asked at the supper table, "did steak go out of circulation when the Democrats went out of office?" What did she say back? "Oh, you're always complaining." Always, eh?

"Sure, I'll be always complaining," you snapped back,

"all the way to the poorhouse. Unless I find some way to make more money to keep you in clover!"

Then it hits you. Why you've been yakking at her and rubbing your money shortages under her skin for the last month. You wish she'd go back to nursing and bring home a paycheck like Joe's wife. Yeah, that's what's been in back of your mind. Why not? She can get a baby-sitter to police the tots and send the biggest one to nursery school. Sure she'll have to drop out of her koffeeklatsch and give up a few of her other favorite pastimes. But so what?

You roll over and begin mentally formulating the speech you'll give her in the morning. But you already know what she'll say. "What about the kids?" And you'll say, "Look at Joe's kids. They leave them with this old woman on Twelfth Street."

"Yeah," she'll say. "Just look at Joe's kids. A couple of crying brats, that's what they are." And she's right, this time. Joe's kids act like they got trouble inside that all the new toys they buy with mom's paycheck just can't reach.

So would it be worth it to you? With twins in diapers and a preschooler who's already insecure?

Alternatives. So shall you tell your wife you think she ought to go back to nursing and bring home another paycheck so you can get ahead financially?

It has its advantages. If she goes back to her profession, your income will rise steeply. Of course, you'll have increased taxes, and if you have preschoolers, she'll have to lay out a good slice of her check to pay for their keep while she's at work, and then there are all the other little inconveniences trying to bend your lives to two working-week schedules. But those aren't really disadvantages.

The real drawback won't be visible on the surface. Not right away. It's the effect it will have on your kids. The price you pay for leaving them in the hands of proxy parents. And the lifelong costs of their insecurity, rejection-reactions and other complications can drain you for the rest of your life—and their lives!

The other alternative? Examine the real issue. Your values. Your priorities. Just how important is financial success to you? How important are all the extras you'd like to have? Worth risking the long-term effects that growing up without parents will have on your kids?

Those are a few of the issues a man's got to face before he lets work scatter his family ten hours a day—just for the benefit of that extra paycheck his wife could bring in.

So what he does will all depend on which values he chooses and whether they're so valuable to him that he can't afford to lose out on family life at its most responsible and most meaningful level.

And if he considers what a family is supposed to be (by checking on the original blueprints from the master Designer—God), he might discover that parenthood is a responsibility that accepts no proxies. It's the sort of commitment which puts people first, even ahead of mink coats and all other dreams.

As you decide. Has your profession been earmarking most of your time, stealing even those few moments you meant to invest in living and life together with those you love?

Or could it be that you've asked for this rat race with no finish line, this work-work-work routine with no letup? You can ask for it by overcommitting yourself financially, by making unrealistic plans, by biting off more than any man—whatever his ability—can chew.

Whatever the reason, you can become a work-aholic. As addicted to slave-driving as a tippler is to his booze or his bender.

Is that possible? Yes indeed it is!

Doctors, counselors, psychiatrists, pastors are all discovering that some of the men we most admire, tireless demons for work, are as sick as the men we most dis-admire, drug addicts and alcoholics.

Dr. Nelson Bradley, chief of psychiatric studies at Lutheran General Hospital in Park Ridge (a suburb of Chicago), says:

> We deplore every other type of addict, but we promote the work addict. We give him status. We accept his estimate of himself. These are our white knights in shining armor: the dynamic executive who is carrying the economy on his shoulders; the newspaperman whose paper will fail if he doesn't meet his deadline; the dedicated doctor who goes on and on—the whole health of the community depends on him, though there are only about fourteen other young doctors who'd love to have part of his practice and who are better trained than he ever was.*

"An unhealthy relationship to work has the same mechanism as an unhealthy relationship to a chemical," agrees Dr. Gordon Bell, of Toronto, an authority on addiction. "And it can be just as self-destructive."†

---

*Nelson Bradley, cited in Alan Phillips, "Work Addiction," *Maclean's* (Canada's National Magazine) (November 4, 1961), pp. 13-14.
†Gordon Bell, cited in ibid.

Overwork is not the disease itself. It is really just the symptom of a deeper problem, of tension, of inadequacy and a need to achieve.

What are the characteristics of the work addict? Most authorities list the following:

He sets the impossible pace and goals which we lightly call the rat race.

He responds to the compulsion to top any and all previous records.

He has no home—his house is only a branch office.

He seldom delegates authority. ("If you want it done right, do it yourself," he says.)

He won't take a vacation but acts so heroic about it.

He can't relax, dislikes weekends, can't wait for Monday.

He makes his own load heavier by bringing more work on himself.

He denies emphatically that he's overworked.

"Put enough pressure on anyone," says Dr. Bradley, "and they'll become addicts."

One man, pushed by the wife he loved, now has everything she wanted, a fifty thousand dollar house, two cars, a maid—and his wife is divorcing him because he is interested only in work. But that will hardly dissuade him. As one work addict put it, "I can always get another wife, but where would I ever find another job like this one?"

And the effect on a work addict's children can be equally disastrous.

"Whether it's through fear or admiration, the work addict molds his children after his own image and insecurity. He can damage their lives as much as an alcoholic," says Dr. Bell. "Not so much because he fails to give them time, but because he never gives himself. They feel rejected."

If he plays with them "it's more in the nature of a ritual," Bradley says. "His behavior is automatic, obligatory."‡

How do we break this work fixation, compulsion, habit, or whatever it is?

"Any change must come from within," Dr. Bradley says. "We can attack addiction with rules about work and vacations, but the only real answer is religion. A new set of values."§

Somehow we must break the endless, vicious circle of overwork. This circle is that: *We want things, and things cost money, and money costs work, and work costs time.* Of course, in the time left over we use the things that cost money. . . .

Can we break this circle of slavery?

No! But Christ can if we let Him master our time, money and work.

Because our problem is a problem of priorities. It's a matter of our basic values being out of skew, and it takes more than just willpower to get one's value system back in line. To establish the right priorities.

If things come first in life, then we will continue to turn all the time we can into money by burning it up in work.

Jesus' values were the exact reverse of this: "Seek . . . first the kingdom of God, and his righteousness; and [then] all these things shall be [yours as well]" (Mt 6:33).

Another time He gave His philosophy of work:

> "You should not work for the food which does not last but for the food which lasts on into eternal life. This is the food the Son of Man will give you, and he is the one who bears the stamp of God the Father."

‡Bradley, cited in ibid.
§Ibid.

> This made them ask him, "What must we do to carry out the work of God?"
>
> "The work of God for you," replied Jesus, "is to believe in the one whom he has sent to you" (Jn 6:27-29, Phillips).

There's a profound insight in those words that you may have missed.

The Master says that if you work only for things—things that are temporary and perishable—your life will be just as transitory. But only a set of values that centers itself in people and their eternal good is worthy of life.

But how do you work that out in life?

May I suggest a simple rule of thumb for determining your priorities in line with Christ's principle? I do not know its original source, but its value has been proven in many lives.

It's a four-word scale.

You must be first a *person*, then a *partner*, then a *parent*, and last of all a *professional*, whatever your profession may be: plumber, painter, politician or preacher.

First, be a *person*. You yourself must become a true person, wholly alive to God and man. You must maintain your personal, spiritual and mental health inviolate so that you can be of service to others. Seek God's kingdom first. In your own heart. As Paul once wrote:

> I run the race then with determination. I am no shadow-boxer; I really fight! I am my body's sternest master, for fear that when I have preached to others I should myself be disqualified (1 Co 9:26-27, Phillips).

Second, be a *partner*. If you choose marriage, it is not meant to be just a convenient way of life. It is a commitment of loyalty that dare not be sold short in the scramble to reach temporary goals. You must build your lives together into a unity of loving respect and mutual concern. As a whole person, be a true partner. The Bible puts it:

> Men ought to give their wives the love they naturally have for their own bodies. The love a man gives his wife is the extending of his love for himself to enfold her (Eph 5:28-29, Phillips).

Third, be a *parent*. Your children are your unique responsibility. If you fail in guiding and molding their lives, you fail them, yourself and your greatest responsibility in life.

Fourth and last place goes to being a *professional*. To your work and its demanding schedule. Where it threatens to absorb your time, crowd out the other priorities in your life, a clear insight into your own values can set things straight right at the outset.

Whatever the temptation to develop work addiction, you can break it. Put first things first.

Let God be God in your life. Then, be a person; be a partner; be a parent; and lastly, be a professional.

In that order. And only that order!

6

On Stepping Out

Scene one. So you're on your way back from the diner to your pullman car. And there, three paces from your roomette, is a lady's purse. Expensive! There's a crack of light showing from a nearby compartment, so you knock. The brunette who opens the door—well, you look twice to make sure she's real. She's smiling and reaching out for the purse you still hold, forgotten.

"Where did you get that?" she asks in mock alarm.

"Out here on the hall floor," you reply.

"It must have tumbled out when I closed the door," she says. "What a tragedy for me if you hadn't come along." You smile your best, and then she adds suggestively, "If there's any way I can say thank you—"

Back in your roomette, you suddenly think of a way. Maybe she's lonely too? A visit perhaps? On a train, in the night, who would ever know? Certainly not your wife. And the girl needn't know your name, so there's no possibility of a kickback. You pause, hand on latch. Should I—should I not?

Shall you follow the pulse hammering in your veins, the hunger in your blood? Or recall the loyalty you owe your wife?

Alternatives. The easiest? Go knock on her door once more. Suggest an appropriate way for her to say thank you. She looks like she just stepped out of one of your daydreams. And, like in the dreams, there are no involvements. She'll pass like a train in the night. Who will ever know? Why not take advantage of the moment?

But before you go, why not have a look at the disadvantages? Even if it's worth the risk of her refusing and complaining to the conductor, is it worth what it will do to the relationship between you and your wife? Cheating like that has a way of changing things a bit. You'll be less honest, less genuine, in your expressions of love to her. You won't feel quite as clean inside. All this adds up to regrets, doesn't it? Then consider what it will do to the girl. Maybe she is "that kind," but a rendezvous with you won't make her any better a person. You'll be using her. That's not the kind of man you want to be. That's the real question, isn't it? What kind of man do you want to be?

The other alternative is to forget her. Remember your wife instead. Disadvantages? You'll have to be alone. Cool down, read the paper, and forget the moment's temptation. You sleep tonight with a clear conscience and get off the train in the morning without looking over your shoulder. You face your wife with honesty in your eye and the increased love you'll know because you've thought of her instead. You can talk to your kids without feeling something like a traitor.

And what's more, you're honest before God. He's interested in you and your wife, in the two of you making a beautiful thing of your marriage; He made you that way, remember?

Scene two. So you're back in your hotel room after the evening session of the convention, the night is young, and the city lights sparkle invitingly across your twelfth-floor view. You're kicking yourself for getting tied up in that discussion group and getting left behind when your gang went out on the town. Then you remember the card. You dig it out of your wallet. Yeah, there it is, the card with a phone number. Bud Wilson gave it to you as he checked out on Tuesday.

You've known Bud ever since you worked together in the same branch office back in Des Moines. Your wives had been great friends, but you hadn't seen him in several years. Big-talking sort of guy. And when he got on his favorite subject—girls—the tales were even bigger. Not that you believed any of it, until you ran into him at the checkout desk.

"Here," he says, slipping a card into your coat pocket, "a contact for the sharpest girl you ever saw in your life. Just dial this number and ask the guy that answers for Sherrie, then give him your room number. Then in about twenty minutes, there'll be this little knock on the door; and when you open it, you won't believe your eyes. But you'll start believing. You bet you will."

You look at the card again, then at the phone by your bed. This is a little out of your league. Cheat on your wife? That you've never done, except in your mind. But what'll it hurt to dial the number and see if Bud is more than a bag of hot air? Picking up the phone, you tell yourself, *After all, it's probably the number for the police department or homicide, or maybe it's dial-a-prayer.* That reminds you. If Bud isn't joking, what will you do? Your conscience isn't quite trusting you.

Then the answer. A man's voice saying, "Yes?"

"May I speak to Sherrie?" you ask.

"Sherrie isn't available just now. May I have her call you?"

Then you've got to decide. So old Bud was telling the truth—now what do you do? Take the call girl—or call it off right now by hanging up?

Alternatives. Shall you give the guy your room number and see if Bud was right about her being the sharpest girl you've ever seen in your life? At night, in a hotel, in the big city, when all your buddies are out on the town— who could see, who would ever know? And there are no involvements with a call girl—no sticky ties you can't cut. After it's over, she walks out the door and that's it.

But before you give him the number, why not let your conscience—or your common sense, whichever you call it— tick off the disadvantages.

Even if it's worth the money, what will it do to the relationship with your wife? You'll feel less honest, be less genuine in your expressions of love to her. Call it what you choose, an affair—even a forty-minute one—is cheating.

And is it worth the hangover of possible regrets? The feeling of having used another person who didn't mean a thing to you—used her like a "thing."

That's not the kind of man—like Bud—that you really want to become, is it?

There's always the other alternative. Hang up on the guy and dial your wife instead. No, she won't be able to come knocking, but tell her how much you love her, that she means more than—well, you tell her.

It'll leave you feeling honest, genuine, clear in conscience, right with your family and yourself.

Of course that takes strength. The strength of love, the courage of conviction, and the kind of character that Jesus Christ can build into any man who lets Him. And that's something you'll want to choose for yourself too.

Scene three. You're on the job painting—lonely job—and you're thinking out loud. Got to keep yourself company, only right now you're not such good company.

"Once more up this ladder and the high part'll be done. Then I'll trim those windows and—

"Ah, this paint! Thick as molasses. But I got a lot of dirt to cover. I'll just spread it on thick."

Then your conscience breaks in to ask, *You've been doing a lot of that lately, haven't you?*

"Sure, that's my job, cover-up man. Something looks bad, slap on another coat of paint."

And that's what you've been trying to do at home too, isn't it? All those gifts and nice words to your wife and kids—it's just painting over that affair with Rita. Be extra nice; the wife'll never suspect, eh?

"Forget it, will you? Painting's lonely enough without having your conscience on your back."

Come on. Cut the arguing and face yourself. Man, you can't keep spreading it on thick, hoping to cover up your double-dealing forever. Things are liable to blow sky-high. Man, we've gotta straighten it out!

"Whataya know? I'm outa paint."

And you're out of more than paint. You're out of defenses, out of excuses. And your common sense keeps on bugging you about that little "friendship" with Rita. What can you do with it?

Alternatives. Shall you keep on with this miserable covering up, or try to silence that nagging conscience once for all?

Come to think of it, how do you shut off an irritating conscience? By ignoring it? Hardly. By trying to put it out of commission? No. As described in chapter 4, 20 percent of it is the scale of right and wrong; 30 percent of it is worry; and the rest is just old-fashioned common sense. Can't turn that off!

Shall you just keep on painting it over with self-justification, hoping you'll be able to cover it up indefinitely? Yes, if you're either an optimist or a magician.

But that won't help you live with yourself. The longer the affair with Rita runs, the harder it will be to break it off. And varnishing it over any longer will only make the hurt—back at your home—a lot deeper. You've got to take a frank look at the barrier it's building between you and your wife. And there's the distance between you and your kids that seems to be stretching wider and wider.

Maybe you ought to reach some agreement with Rita and say good-bye. At least start being an honest man again for a change.

Would you have to open it up with your wife? That might hurt more than it would heal. Maybe you should just live your apology to her. Show her you care. If she doesn't know about it already, that could be a lot kinder than hitting her with the story.

You've got to do *something*! The kind of life you're living is only a half-life, a secretive shadow of what a full-blown, honest kind of life could be. The kind of life God could begin building for you right now if you'd let Him. If you accept His forgiveness for the past and His strength for a new kind of life in the future, then you could really make it right with your wife, and make it up to her in the future!

As you decide. Think long. Think hard. Think carefully about the nature of your commitment, your covenant of marriage. Think deeply about the nature of sexuality, fidelity, loyalty, and integrity.

Most men avoid those long thoughts. They just assume that they'll always be good, faithful husbands; and then, in a thoughtless moment when pressures are high and resistance is low, they break. And so does their integrity.

In that moment of temptation, many a man's better sense lets him down because he has never done a bit of ahead-of-time thinking about the case for being faithful or the causes and consequences of being unfaithful.

What are the causes? Obviously they're as varied as people. But whatever the causes, they all go right back to the four basic reasons for any and all sexual relations. Three of the reasons, though prevalent and popular, are invalid. Only one is either adequate or justifiable.

The first cause of sex relations is experimentation. Youth may feel a great deal of curiosity, wondering what sex is like and what it's all about. So they're tempted to experiment. But would you believe that many married men talk themselves into justifying extramarital relations as a necessary experiment? "I just had to find out," they insist. "I had to know if this or that was true."

A second reason is sexual desire. Sexual drives in themselves are natural and necessary. But like all other motivating forces in man, they must be controlled constructively and channeled into creative purposes.

The misuse of sex desires as "recreation" uses the other

person as only a body. It is not fulfillment, just release. Not the shared joy of two fully human persons, a joy consecrated by intimate and infinite devotion, but the mechanical tripping of a safety valve to release pressure. This divorces the sex act from all creative forces of personhood, leaving an individual emotionally drained, mentally defeated, and spiritually depressed. The jaded Romans quoted an old Latin proverb, "After intercourse all animals are sad." Sex, abused by misuse, always leaves behind an empty sadness.

But when it creatively nourishes love, love in the all-exclusive commitment of marriage, it is not sad but excruciatingly joyful, beautiful, unifying, and mutually fulfilling.

A third reason for sex relations is escape. Ninety-nine out of every hundred adulteries are vain attempts at escape.

Infidelity, like alcoholism or drug addiction, is an expression of the undesirable character trait of indecisive weakness, or of evasion of straight dealing in shallow dishonesty, or a misguided attempt to escape.

If you are tempted to be untrue to your wife, ask yourself, "What am I trying to escape? What frustration, jealousy, insecurity, defeat, self-pity, self-doubt, or inadequacy lies behind my obsession?"

Sex relations outside marriage are almost never motivated by physical desire. That is only the mechanics of the final act.

Extramarital sex is a symptom, an unconscious confession of emptiness, an admission of a great lack. It may be a lack of success, of importance, of personal fulfillment, or ability to be truly intimate with another. So sex becomes an escape. A momentary narcotic. A crutch for a crippled ego. Extramarital sex is a symptom of defeated, futile living.

The fourth reason—and the only valid one—for sex relations is love. Not the love of what you get from another, but the love which compels you to give without reservation. Sex is the action which demonstrates the utter self-abandoning of two persons pledged to unconditional intimacy, loyalty, and *fidelity*. Such love never demands sex as a free gift or a momentary loan. Such love exists only in a mutual state of self-giving in which each exists for the other. Its name is marriage.

Sex acts outside marriage have no true meaning—however emotional the participants may be—because they attempt to symbolize a total giving of oneself at a time when a state of complete giving—marriage—does not exist.

These are the causes behind all sex relations. Experimentation, escape, sexual desire, or selfless love. Only one is valid. Only one is creative. Only one brings fulfillment, security, stability, maturity, integrity, and all the other gifts of life.

That one is the fidelity of love.

Infidelity involves so much more than just extramarital sex. It is a denial of love, a betrayal of trust, a refusal to your mate's total faith and confidence. It is disloyalty and dishonesty of life.

The late Swiss theologian Emil Brunner wrote, "Marriage is based not so much on love as on fidelity." Think about that. It's true, isn't it? The very basis of your marriage is the absolute commitment of life without reservation. To break fidelity is to break the bonds of marriage itself.

The Lord Jesus Christ said: "Every man who looks at

a woman lustfully has already committed adultery with her—in his heart" (Mt 5:28, Phillips).

Paul asks,

> Have you forgotten that the kingdom of God will never belong to the wicked? Don't be under any illusion—neither the impure, . . . or the adulterer . . . shall have any share in the kingdom of God. Our physical body was [not] made for sexual promiscuity; it was made for God, and God is the answer to our deepest longings.
>
> Avoid sexual looseness like the plague! Every other sin that a man commits is done outside his own body, but this is an offense against his own body. Have you forgotten that your body is the temple of the Holy Spirit, who lives in you, and is God's gift to you, and that you are not the owner of your own body? You have been bought, and at what a price! Therefore bring glory to God in your body (1 Co 6:9-10, 13b, 18-20, Phillips).

7

Why Get Involved?

Scene one. You're having lunch down at Luigi's, talking business with one of your fellow workers (actually, you're chewing out the boss) when the real estate agent who sold you your house stops by the table. You introduce him to your friend. "He's the fellow who sold me my castle," you say. "Great guy, great house he got for me." Then the guy says it.

"You heard about your new neighbors?"

"No," you say. "You mean that house next door is sold?"

"Yeah," he says, "not by us, of course. That other agency had it!"

"What about the neighbors?" you ask.

He gives you a long slow look; then he spills it. "They're Negroes," he says.

"Negroes," you say in disbelief. "Uh, now don't get me wrong," you say, "I believe in integration, open housing, and all that. I'm not prejudiced. But our neighborhood's different. Man, what'll that do to the value of my place?"

"Can't say," he replies. "In six weeks, after they've moved

in, it could drop a couple thousand. In six months, who knows? You might be wise to get out before the rush."

"The rush?" you ask in shock.

"Sure," he says. "The rush when everybody else is selling to the first buyer. You see, I could advertise it today yet. Sell it for you before the news breaks—if you can keep it mum."

"So you'd sell if you were me," you say. "If I decide to do anything, I'll give you a ring." Then you're left wondering what to do. You'd sure hate to move now. And your wife. She's had all the moving she can take. But you can't afford to lose a couple grand. If you stay, maybe the value won't drop. Yeah, but if everybody tries to sell at once, everything's gone! Maybe you could organize the block and deal with the threat some other way. What shall you do?

Alternatives. Should you sell? A phone call and you'll be the first of the white exodus.

Oh, but will your wife like that! You've already moved her twice too often.

But why run? The new neighbors won't be lowering any prices. It's the crash selling craze that does it. Why not stay? Tell the rest of your block about the new people and enlist them to stay and put their actions where they say their opinions are when they're talking liberally over coffee cups. If only everyone stays put—and who wants to move —there will be no change in values at all.

Or maybe you'd lean toward trying to keep the new folks out of the neighborhood. There are a lot of ways that have been tried. If you've a rich friend with prejudice to spend, have him buy them out.

Or you could always find a way to pass on a threat or

two. That has a way of discouraging newcomers. Or certainly there are other ways.

Or maybe you could ask, What's the human thing, the right thing, to do? If you treat another man as a thing, you're not a human being yourself anymore. You've become a thing, too. After all, you were created to be a true man—compassionate, fair and concerned about your neighbor—whatever his color—as well as yourself. How was it Christ put it? "Love the Lord God with all your heart, and your neighbor as yourself."

Scene two. So you and your wife are having dinner out with your brother-in-law and his spouse. (He's a big cheese in the city, council member and professional committee-sitter.) And he's telling you about the hassle they had today in city council.

It seems two of the men who represent the junk-side of town—slums, ghetto and funny-people land—were asking for an appropriation to go on a rat-killing program.

"Imagine," your brother-in-law says, slapping the table, "these people expect us to pay for exterminating the rats they've been raising with all their garbage. And that's what I said to the whole proposal, garbage! They grow their own rats, they can kill 'em."

You push your peas and carrots around the plate with your fork, trying to get up the courage to tell him. Tell him that you know what it's like to hear rats in the room—the scratch of their feet, the squeaks and squeals in the night, their tiny nails on the floors as they scrounge the house for food.

But would he remember those depression days when the rats multiplied in the poor housing area where your families lived? Would he remember how dads lined their kiddies' cribs with old window screening to protect them from rat bite? No, apparently his memory doesn't go back that far across the tracks. So there were fifteen thousand cases of rat bite in our cities last year, but why should you try to rub it in? Why argue with the guy? He's always right; you'll only louse up the evening and mess up your friendship for a couple weeks.

And yet, you can't let this go by. That council owes their assistance in wiping out the city's rats, right? But it's his prejudice, his bigotry, his apathy standing in the way. So, shall you tell him and risk his irritation? Or swallow your own convictions and grunt some agreeable sounds?

Alternatives. If you buck his point of view, he'll turn against you just like you've seen him do to others who fought his pet policies. Why ask for trouble?

And he's on the city council, not you. Certainly he may have more facts, he might know something you don't know.

Maybe it gets to you where you can't shut it off. Maybe you feel a little angry about the babies that have been rat bait in your town. Maybe you feel that someone has got to care! And if the city council doesn't or won't, then who will? Somebody's got to take the leadership in cleaning out the menace. Why not tell him—straight between the eyes. Let him know how one loyal constituent feels!

Or, maybe you could soft-pedal it a little. Just give him your views, without arguing, and avoid any steamed words, if that's possible.

Or maybe you could just ask him enough questions to make him uncomfortable about it. Who knows, if you ask him the right questions, it might set him thinking in a few new ways, help him see his prejudice, feel his bias. That would be worth a lot!

Well, what you choose to do when your view isn't the popular one at the moment is up to you. If you set your principles and values by what is accepted by important people around you, then the answer will be easy.

But if concern for others' welfare or compassion for those who are deprived gets through to you, if being a real human matters much, if refusing to accept either prejudging or prejudice is important, then you'll have to do something, say something, or even stick your neck out for what you know to be just and right. Why would you do that? Could be because that was Christ's way—to love your neighbor as yourself. Can you give a better reason?

Scene three. So you just heard the shouts of these kids in the park across the street, ran to the window, and then you spotted it all. It looks like the gang from six blocks uptown is having a blast beating up the kids from your block. You watch, fascinated, but then it turns even rougher. One of the kids is apparently getting more than he can take. He's shouting, fist shaking; then you see light flash on metal. A knife. Now the guys form a circle. Someone throws a switchblade to the other guy, and they begin an awkward dance, backing around the ring, knives glinting. "Those cops better get here fast," you say, "or it'll be a hearse we'll be needing instead."

Then you wonder. Has anyone called the cops? Not you, that's for sure. They're black, you're white. You don't make a practice out of getting your nose into these racial things. But all the neighbors must be watching. Certainly someone has called.

By now the boys have closed in. The knives dart in and

out. You lift the window a bit, listening for the siren, but no sound.

There, the one boy's holding his arm. He's cut, yet the fighting and knife thrusts go on. The others are shouting like murder. You turn to go for the phone, then you hesitate. Why get involved? You've no legal responsibility to run for the cops. So what do you do? You can't stand by much longer and see that kid get stuck or killed.

Alternatives. The fight is obviously in its last desperate moments. If the police don't arrive in a moment, it will be too late for at least one kid.

Shall you phone the emergency police number? There's likely a squad car within a block. There could be help here before it's too late.

But then, you've never called the cops before. Sure you're on the side of law and order, but do you have to get involved, get summoned to witness in court and all that?

But even though you're slow to call the police, does that mean you must stand by uninvolved? It would only take a minute down the elevator, thirty seconds to cross the street. An adult yell with a few authoritative gestures might break it up—or turn both gangs back on you. Well, you've got the safety of your apartment to dash back to.

Or you could grab your neighbor across the hall to go along out. But wait, why try to play police yourself? Why not give them the call?

Well, what you do is all up to you. But *why* you are hesitating is the real issue. Is it your feeling of racial superiority that lets you overlook human need? Could it be your prejudice that tells you to forget it and let those blacks do their own thing? You a bigot who looks the

other way when a kid may be dying? No, that's not you—
or is it?

As you decide. Consider the one absolutely unprejudiced
man who ever lived, the one person who offered personal,
social, spiritual and moral help in conquering prejudice.

Jesus Christ!

"Now wait," you may say, "the followers of Christ are
among the most prejudiced people in our nation." Yes,
some of them are.

For some people, religious faith becomes a scaffold to
buttress their own biases and bigotry. Assuming that our
God is obviously "our kind" or He would be neither "ours"
nor "God," they reject the very truth of God in sincere but
tragic blindness. (How often a man may be at his worst
when at his most religious moments.) But when a man
allows his faith in Christ to stand in judgment over all his
actions and reactions, prejudice shows up in a very harsh
light.

"Now wait," you ask, "haven't you just admitted that religion makes some people bigoted and intolerant, yet you
insist it makes others more understanding, caring and accepting? How can this be?"

Could it be that those who *use* religion—for status, security or social opportunity—accept only the parts of religion that reinforce their own views?

But those who, in faith, commit themselves unreservedly
to follow Jesus Christ in life find something else? Can it
be that they find a new strength in Christ to love their
neighbor? Or a new pattern in Christ of what it means to
be a human being to fellow humans, a child of God to all
His other children? Can it be that as they die to prejudice,
as Christ promised, they are born again to a life of love?

To find the answer, look at Jesus Christ. Look long with the eyes of both your mind and your heart.

He was born in the most rigidly ethnic culture of all time; born in a fiercely nationalistic nation; born in Galilee, the most bigoted backwoods area of that nation; born into a family of snobbish royal lineage; born in a time when revolutionary fanaticism fired every heart with hatred for the Roman oppressors; born in a country practicing the apartheid of rigid segregation between Jews and Samaritans.

Yet He showed not a trace of it.

I challenge you to read and reread the documents of His life. There is nothing, absolutely nothing, that you can find to indicate any feelings of racial superiority, national prejudice or personal discrimination.

He taught "Love thy neighbor as thyself." He lived it. "Greater love hath no man than this," He once said, "that a man lay down his life for his friends" (Jn 15:13). He did it. He summed up His goals in life with these words:

> The Spirit of the Lord is upon me.
> He has anointed me to preach the Good News to the poor,
> He has sent me to proclaim liberty to the captives,
> And recovery of sight to the blind,
> To set free the oppressed,
> To announce the year when the Lord will save his people!
>
> (Lk 4:18-19, TEV)

He died for it.

Died as the victim of man's prejudiced hatreds. Shadowed by scared-into-inaction disciples. Sentenced at a trial without defense. Condemned by those who had pre-judged Him by their own prejudices. Executed by the bigotry and selfishness of man.

Those who stand on the side of Jesus Christ reject prej-udice whenever, however and wherever they find it. In themselves first of all; then and only then in the world about them.

"No man can know Christ truly except he follow Him daily in life" (Hans Denk). A life of love. A life of for-giveness. A life of acceptance. As Jesus Christ lived, loved and died.

Would you like the release from prejudice that Jesus Christ gives?

First, *know Him truly.* Surrender all the sins of selfish-ness that control and contain you. He will free you and forgive you. What's more, He will inhabit your life with His loving self and His own strength to love.

Then, *follow Him daily in life.* An unprejudiced life of concern for others.

What will this mean? Friend-making. Across racial lines. Why should you have only white (or brown or yel-low) friends? Why advance the cause of prejudice by limiting your friendships to "your kind"?

Share the joy of your faith in Christ with others—of any race or place. Let Christ be the Christ of your life, words, deeds.

It will mean going where the barriers are. Refuse to go to a one-race-only church. Avoid restaurants and busi-nesses that serve only one kind of people. Welcome fam-ilies of other races to move into your block. If you employ, hire on the basis of actual qualifications only, not phony fears of color problems.

If you say you love your neighbor, live it. As Jesus did. Without prejudging or prejudice.

8

Who Says Talk Is Cheap?

Scene one. Who was it told the story first? Oh yeah, Bill Speck, who works back on the punch press. It seems he was visiting some friends in this town about fifty miles west last Sunday afternoon, and they all decide to go out to the restaurant for supper. Well, they're sitting there chatting when who comes in but our foreman, Lou Sefcheck, with this blonde on his arm, and, wow, what a dream she is.

Bill does a double take, then buries his face in the menu while Sefcheck goes by. It's not his wife, that's for sure. This broad's too young, and he wouldn't be fawning over her that way. They get a table back in the corner, and does Bill ever have a time watching them. Got three gravy stains on his tie from missing his mouth.

So, too good a chance to miss—he excuses himself and goes by their table on his way to the men's room. On the way back, he stops, claps the foreman on the back and says loudly, "Why, Mr. Sefcheck, fancy meeting you here, and with your lovely wife."

"Sorry, sir," Sefcheck says stiffly, "but you got the wrong man. My name's William Jones."

"Oh, pardon me, Mr. Jones," says Bill, "but I could have sworn you were Lou Sefcheck, foreman at Carbide Steel Works. Wait till I tell him tomorrow at coffee break that I saw his double."

Well, so Sefcheck hasn't shown up in coffee break for a week. Speck's been sitting on the story, but today he let it slip to you. He said, "It's my policy never to say anything about anyone unless it's something good, and boy is this good."

Yeah, so it is, but will it be good for Sefcheck? Or if it spreads, as you know it will, will it be good for his marriage?

So what's it to you? Well, you can either pass it on and enjoy the laughs, or you could go back to Speck, see if there isn't some way to save all the trouble this could cause for a lot of people.

Alternatives. What shall you do about the good story that's just about to break?

Go ahead and enjoy it? It's going to be an all-time great laugh for the guys in the factory. But not for Sefcheck. So, it may teach him a lesson. But good.

Or maybe you ought to go talk to Speck? Tell him you think it was great the way he sat on the story for a week. Suggest he might want to do it permanently and give Sefcheck a break.

Or he could go talk to Sefcheck in his office. Tell him he'll sit on the story if the boss gets him off that punch press and gives him a promotion to the next department. Why throw away a bargaining card like this one just for laughs?

Or maybe Speck would consider it another way. This could be his chance to help Sefcheck think about where this two-timing play will take him. He might be able to help the guy take a big step in the right direction that could help his wife, his kids, his whole life.

Well, what he does with the story will be up to him, but your choice is still right there in your hands. Shall you spread the story around, or do something with it that you won't regret later?

What you do with good prime gossip can make a crucial difference for you and for the guy on the other end of it.

If you don't mind being destructive—and what can be more destructive than an explosive story—then pass it on. But if you value the sort of things that are constructive, that help your fellowmen build their lives in a better direction, then gossip won't help anybody. If there were a golden rule on this, wouldn't it go: "Never pass on anything about somebody that you wouldn't want anybody to pass on about you"?

If you could do that, you'd be taking a first step toward loving your neighbor as yourself, as Christ recommended.

Scene two. "Hey, I've got to tell you this," a friend of yours says to you at coffee break. "Now don't get me wrong and don't get mad. I'm only passing it on because I think you oughta know, see?"

"Sure," you grunt. "So why all the introduction. We're friends, aren't we? So I got bad brea—"

"No, no," he says, "it's something worse! You see, there's this story going round the shop about you. I thought you ought to get it straight now, before it goes too far."

"OK. Let's have it," you say.

"Well," he says, "it isn't too pretty. I picked it up yesterday back in the parts department. It seems you took this weekend fishing trip—you and your wife, that is—with Jim Smith and his wife, right? Well, last weekend Smith took one of the other guys and his wife along up to this cabin, and today this guy says Smith gave him a selling pitch on swapping wives for the weekend. This guy says nothing doing, told Smith to shut his face up about it or they were going home that night yet. And Smith tells him to come off it, he doesn't need to act so righteous. Why, just the week before when you and he swapped wives, you told him that this other guy was an old hand at it. So Smith says, it was just a case of mistaken information from you."

"Why, that rat," you say. "We did no such thing, and I never— He's just trying to weasel out of his embarrassing spot by spreading the blame all around and justifying himself. You just wait till I get close to that Smith."

"Now, you better cool it too," your buddy says. "Flying off the handle and smearing him one will only make you look guilty of everything. You gotta handle this smart or else you'll wind up with more people believing it than if you do nothing at all."

"Well, you don't expect me to stand by with my mouth shut while every guy in the plant is laughing behind my back, do you?"

"No," he says, "I just said act smart, that's all."

That's when coffee break ended, and then you're back on the job wondering what to do. How do you stop a gossip smear?

Alternatives. Shall you go slug him one, right in the shop? Hardly. You'd get in trouble with the boss, and then who'd ever believe that you were innocent? Only a guilty guy would lose his head like that.

You could look for him after work. Catch him where no one's likely to see; give him a couple threats, or bust his lip. But he's a pretty big guy, and what's worse, he could use that story against you too, and it would be true. And it might confirm the other one, too.

Maybe you should confront him in front of all the guys at coffee break tomorrow. Get the whole mess right out on the table. Yeah, but if the guy can fabricate a story on the spot to get himself out of a jam with one guy, who knows what lie he'll tell in front of the crowd.

Or should you see your lawyer? See if you've got a good slander case waiting to be exploited?

Maybe you better just shut up on it all. You can set anybody straight who comes and asks you. Hopefully the guys who know you won't believe it anyway. Why worry about the others? They don't really matter that much to you.

Should you and your wife go and talk with his family and lay things on the line? After all, their real problem isn't just this gossip. They've got deeper troubles that are crying for help.

Could be you could offer some help, or tell them where to find it. Tell them that their marriage could be a beautiful thing if they'd let it shape up like a marriage was designed to be. By the great Designer who intended us to live by a real kind of love—His kind.

And what about the rumor? Whatever you do about it, shouldn't it be done out of concern for the other guy as well as for your own reputation? Isn't that where God's kind of love comes in? To love your neighbor as yourself? Even if he's a gossip?

Scene three. You've just come back from coffee break

and this guy, Fred, has set you thinking. Just a crack or two he made after all the jokes had been told, jokes on the standard three topics—sex, sex and—sex. Then this guy, Fred, said—and you can still hear him—he said, "It's mighty hard for me to believe, but they tell me there are still a few guys around who stick to one woman all their life. I'd like to meet one," he continued, "and see what kind of fool he is. Why, everybody knows that variety is the spice of life. Or should I have said the spice of *wife*?" he added. Then he broke into a horselaugh at his gag. The other guys all laughed and you suddenly realized you were laughing along too.

Now that you're back at your machine, his words begin to rankle you. *Why do I buy all this stuff? Why don't I walk away from this, or even say something to the guys? Why do we always have to make with the wife-trading stuff?* You begin to wonder why you don't tell Fred to cut it out, but what would you tell him? That you love your wife? That she's so lovely—and loving—that you, well, you can't imagine even wanting someone else? You'd tell him you can spot a pretty knee as fast as the next man, but that doesn't mean you start panting. But would he understand? Or would he believe you?

You're not sorry that you've always been faithful to your wife, but now can you explain why? Shouldn't you tell this Fred guy why?

What *are* the reasons? Reasons a man can respect?

Alternatives. You could ignore him. Take your coffee break elsewhere. Avoiding him could save a lot of embarrassment. The fellows seem to get a lot of laughs out of his stuff. They'd get double humor at your expense as he painted you as some special sort of square.

But he's been asking for it, day after day. He deserves to be told. You can hardly run away. So tomorrow you'll tell him. But how?

You could begin by leveling. Tell him that you think any man worth his salt is a man who keeps faith with his wife, who works at making his marriage *great*, and doesn't even *think* about stepping out. Tell him that any man who will cheat on his wife without a second thought, and laugh at those who don't, doesn't know the first thing about integrity—or real marriage. But those are fighting words. True, and painful ones too. He'll have to strike back with all he's got.

Maybe you could sneak up on his blind side. Next time he's sounding off about "every man ought to play the field, get all he can," ask him "Who was that dark-haired man your wife was out with last week?" Then watch him flare, watch the anger bubble up, then spring it on him. Say, "See there. You don't believe this free love stuff at all— not for your wife at least—nobody except you. If you're so sold on sleeping all around, why get worked up over a rumor about your wife?" Then tell him, "Want to know who the man was? Maybe you!" Might work if he hears you out before belting you one.

Or why don't you tell him your real reason for being faithful to your wife? Tell him you believe in loyalty. That's the stuff that makes life worth living. Tell him you believe in fidelity. It's the cement that holds marriages together. Tell him you believe in integrity. Tell him you believe in your wife—no chance, however easy, can tempt you to sacrifice all she means to you for a few moments with some other dame. Tell him that as far as you're concerned, sex isn't worth it outside marriage. Chasing broads can be just a mechanical-bunny chase. But inside marriage, where there's true respect, intimacy, fidelity, integrity and unity of spirit, sex means something deep. Something worth a lifetime.

Above all, tell him that the life you're enjoying gives you that solid feeling of permanence, because you're living it like God meant it to be lived—both you and your wife. And, knowing and following Jesus Christ as you do, you wouldn't want it any other way. No reserve—you're enjoying it all the way, and no regrets. It doesn't go sour.

Sure, you could tell him all that. If it's real to you and you mean it. If you've found it true. And no matter how he takes it—or what he says—he'll have to hear you out, and respect you, too.

As you decide. Why not refuse to listen to any conversation that begins with any of these old lines: "Oh, by the way, have you heard the rumor that . . ."; "I just got it from an inside source that . . ."; "Don't say I told you, but they say that . . ."; "Did you hear the latest about . . .?"; "Everybody knows. You mean you hadn't heard yet?"; "Oh, it's just too awful for words, but I've got to tell you. You ought to know."

The topic? Probably people. People with or without problems. The reason? Gossip. Man's—and woman's—favorite pastime. It's the expected thing. Like the husband answering the phone saying, "I'm sorry but Mrs. Smith is out. Would you care to leave a rumor?"

What about gossip? Is it permissible?

Why do we gossip? Is it justifiable?

What should we do about gossip, gossiping and gossipers?

Let's examine these questions together for a few moments. Since all of us do a bit of gossiping in our spare moments, it may be well worth our time.

What about gossip? Is it ever right? Or never right?

In defense of gossip, psychologist Dr. Joyce Brothers declared:

> Gossip lubricates the gears of the social engine. It's a harmless reliever of tension, an ice breaker, a remarkably effective—and painless—way to transmit substantial quantities of information. As for being malicious—sometimes it is, of course. But that's only when abused. Most gossip is simply what the dictionary says it is, 'Idle talk, not always true, about other people and their affairs."*

Margaret Carson, in an article entitled "Just Gossip? The Case for Woman Talk," goes a step further to sing its praise. She writes:

> Just as chit chat about our own concerns may release pent-up feelings, or help us think through decisions, talking about other people's business allows us to ponder the problems we may some day meet to gain some inkling of the emotional content of these problems. We need to base our decisions on feeling as well as knowing. And it is the "feel" of the situations that gossip gives.†

Well, that's another point of view, yet somehow even the best that is said for gossip is a bit self-incriminating.

When is gossip an innocent lubricant for the gears of social life? Is it ever truly innocent?

Gossiping about another's actual or supposed problem rarely gives us a valid insight into life and living. Certainly gossip inspires feelings, but they're feelings of superior-

---

*Joyce Brothers, *Quote* (November 19, 1967).
†Margaret Carson, *Quote* (October 2, 1966).

ity, not sympathy, or else the story would stop with us. No, in most gossip, there's more enmity than empathy. Like the husband asking his wife, "Say, have you heard the latest about Myrtle?" "Heard it?" she replies, "I started it."

Why do we gossip? We gossip because it does something for us. Something we're not too willing to name and face, but something that makes us feel good—for the moment.

Which should reveal to us that gossip is actually a symptom of emotional disturbance. The knocker, complainer, belittler or gossiper is sick. People who make trouble are generally troubled people.

People gossip to anesthetize their own guilt feelings by pointing out others who are supposedly worse than they.

Or to scapegoat others for faults they find difficult to own up to or they are trying to cover up in themselves.

Or to fulfill their own wishes and desires in imagination since they cannot or will not do them in act.

Gossip is a moral problem for both the talker and the listener. It takes two to gossip. The listener is just as guilty as the speaker. No real man can stand by while an absent and likely innocent person is dirtied. It is a human responsibility to protest the smearing of a fellow human. Why not gently say, "I'd rather not listen to the criticism of another when he's not present to defend himself." Or ask, "Why do you think I should be told this story about him or her?"

Gossip is nothing to toy with. It's desperately serious. It poisons the gossiper, prejudices the listener, and ambushes the victim. It leads to envy, anger, malice, suspicion, violence and murder. It obviously invalidates all personal claims to a principled life.

The Bible says: "If any one appears to be 'religious' but cannot control his tongue, he deceives himself and we may be sure that his religion is useless" (Ja 1:26, Phillips).

And the Bible has a lot more to say about this. It puts gossip among the chief of sins, alongside of lying, stealing, adultery and murder, because it can be all of these in the heart and on the tongue (see Mt 15:19; Ro 1:24-32; Col 3:5-9).

Or listen to what Paul wrote to Christians at Galatia.

> For, dear brothers, you have been given freedom: not freedom to do wrong, but freedom to love and serve each other. For the whole Law can be summed up in this one command: "Love others as you love yourself." But if instead of showing love among yourselves you are always critical and catty, watch out! Beware of ruining each other (Gal 5:13-15, Living N.T.).

But Jesus saw most deeply and warned most sharply. Listen.

> A man's words depend on what fills his heart. A good man gives out good—from the goodness stored in his heart; a bad man gives out evil—from his store of evil. I tell you that men will have to answer at the day of judgment for every careless word they utter—for it is your words that will acquit you, and your words that will condemn you! (Mt 12:34-37, Phillips).

If you know something that would hurt or hinder the life or reputation of another, bury it. Forget it. End it right there. It will rest in peace. So will you.

If you love your neighbor, that love will cover a multitude of sins (1 Pe 4:8).

Love heals. Love encourages. Love protects. Love looks for the best in others so that others may be their best.

The late great Christian, A. W. Tozer, in a message entitled "Five Vows for Spiritual Power," has suggested a way through this problem. "Vow: Never to pass on anything about anybody else that will hurt him in any way."

Wouldn't you like to vow that vow? Now?

9

You're the Driver!

Scene one. You're by yourself on a business trip, running one of those monotonous stretches of interstate. Traffic is light, so you're not exactly concentrating on your driving when you see this—this something—lying on the road in your lane. It's a box. If it's empty, you can just straddle it; but if it's full of something or other it could be rough on a tire or your oil pan. You check the rearview mirror to make sure all's clear behind, then swing the wheel toward the left lane.

In the next split second, the unbelievable happens. As you edge across the broken line, there's the sudden squeal of tires. A car is lurking right in your blind spot. By the time you're aware that he's there, you're against him. Touching? You can never remember. By the time your bumpers should have hooked, you've swung the wheel to the right, begun to skid, twisted the wheel back to correct it. Then, out of the corner of your eye, you see the other car, skidding onto the left shoulder, then hurtling out of control down the median strip, its two wheels along the embankment, then it tips into a quick roll.

You're already braking when it hits you. Must you stop? All the traffic behind you will arrive before you could turn around and go back. They'll give whatever aid is necessary; you're really not needed. You check the mirror again. Certainly no one saw what happened.

If you stop, he could blame it all on you. Why not go on? But would that be hit-and-run? You don't think you actually hit, but it would be leaving the scene of an accident. And if you did touch him, only a scraped fender, a crimped bumper might betray it, and that would prove nothing.

Alternatives. Why not keep on going? Certainly the guy in the other car will get help from the next car that comes along. Someone will likely be to him before you could get stopped and back up.

Why not just forget the whole nightmare. It wasn't any more your fault than his. He hadn't blown his horn. And the guy passing is usually the one in the wrong. And you never touched his car—you think. But then, it happened so fast. If you stop and get out, there may be a swatch of his paint along the side of your car. You won't know until you look.

Could this be hit-and-run? And if the other guy is seriously hurt, that could be complicated. Would you be safer stopping, even though it may be stepping into trouble? Trying to run could be even worse.

You could go back, face up to whatever legal, moral or human responsibility you have in this. It's worth it if you're trying to be a human in an age of machines.

But of course, you may be hopping out of the frying pan into the fire. You'd better know why you're asking for all the red tape and more that owning up to your involvement in the accident may bring.

What reason do you have for acting responsibly when it's voluntary? You were brought up to always face the music? Or maybe you've got the sort of principles that make you look out for the other guy too?

If it's that, it could be that the greatest principle of life has gotten hold of you—the love-your-neighbor-as-yourself principle. Some men do, you know. They do it because once you love the Lord God with all your heart, soul, strength and mind, as Jesus recommended, well, you learn what it is to love your neighbor.

Scene two. So you just eased up on the gas as you approached that eight-sided red sign with a four-letter word, did your usual rolling stop, and took a left through the intersection. You're no sooner in your lane than the air vibrates with the scream of big tires welding themselves to the pavement.

Your eyes lock on the rearview mirror, on the blurred image of the semitruck that is bearing down on you. Your reflexes snap the wheel left, your foot tramps the gas pedal and you feel the pressure of your acceleration pinning you back to your seat.

The split seconds while you see the truck growing larger and larger in your mirror stretch out and you wait for the bone-jarring blow from the rear. Then he thunders by you, not even a scrape on the bumper! There, he's straightened out now and still in his lane, and you're all in the clear.

Your tight stomach muscles soften; you gulp in the air. Sweat stings your eyes, the stiffness of your knees has jellied. You look four directions for a cherry-topped car.

The coasts are clear. Then you sigh in relief, rub your sweaty palms on your trouser legs, and flex your back muscles against the cold trickle of water inching down your spine.

Then you start wondering. Where did he come from? Why didn't I see him? Why do I pull these stupid blunders on the road? What am I thinking about?

Is it worth the few seconds I gain by cutting a few corners, weaving from lane to lane, or out-jumping others at the lights? Here a rolling stop, there a failure to yield right-of-way. If I don't get stopped, if I don't even get a mangled fender—sure, I do shave off a few minutes now and then—so what does it hurt? Or *does* it hurt?

Alternatives. You can keep on driving by the seat of your pants. Your luck has always been good. So why not count on it a little longer?

Or if driving automatically and absentmindedly has begun to worry you a little bit, you could try putting in a little more effort—just so you don't become a driving crank, trailing so many car lengths behind the next guy while the whole world passes you by. Why not just wise up and drive a little more sharply?

Or you could decide to reform your driving, since it is a matter of life and death. If not your life, then perhaps the other guy's. And you can't hope to be the lucky exception forever. Sooner or later, it may be too late.

But driving like a good guy could take all the joy out of your ride. Or don't you gamble at the wheel for the unconscious kicks you get—if you're still conscious?

But let's get to the heart of things. What should be the real reason behind a man's decision on how to drive? Safety? Kicks? Speed? Time-saving? Or concern for others?

After all, caring for people—all people—is the way we men were intended to live. By the original Designer. Is that a reason for driving not just defensively, or responsibly, but respectfully?

Scene three. So this guy is on the final leg of his trip—only fifty miles to go. He's been driving all day, and is he ever anxious to get home. The road is clear and dry, the traffic light. All those horses under his hood are straining to go. His foot slowly descends on the accelerator almost as if it had a will of its own. The needle climbs past the speed limit—10 miles over; 15; 20. What's 75, 80, 85 miles an hour? No harm done.

Then, out of the corner of his eye, the driver sees the gray car pulling out into his lane from a side road. Reflexes take over. Wheel left, brakes pumped; then he sees the truck coming in the other lane. He swings back, tires squealing, brakes clutching at the road. He's overtaking the slow-moving car ahead, he's going into a skid, he's reversed ends, it looks like he may skid past the other car backwards on the wide emergency shoulder. No, his bumper hooks, and both cars careen together, then plunge end over end down the embankment.

Was that your wife in the car he overtook—and took over the bank with him? Was that your wife who paid the price for his speeding?

Or do I have it all reversed? Was that you driving the speeding car? And could it have been the other guy's wife who was tipped over the edge to a bone-shattering crash?

Or don't you speed? "When the road is clear and dry, the traffic light, the hour late and you want to get home."

Alternatives. To speed or not to speed when the pressure's on you, the conditions are good, and the open road is extending its own invitation? You may decide on the advice of your rearview mirror. If there aren't any suspicious-looking cars in view, go ahead and stick your foot into the carburetor. "There's no reason for not speeding if it's safe and you don't get caught." Or is there?

Perhaps you use conditions to decide: good weather, good road, good tires, good clearance in traffic? Is that good enough?

Or do you decide on the basis of your own patience—or impatience? Normally, you hold it down to the rules of the road. But when you're tired, when you've had all the driving you can take, when you just can't wait to get home —then you pour it on.

Or perhaps, like most of us, you consider yourself something of an exception? Sure, you believe in speed limits for others. Sure, you're in favor of careful driving—by the other guy. Sure, you're aware that accidents do happen— to others—so you sit on your seat belts. You're the exception.

So why not speed? Or can it be that responsible citizenship would call you to respect even a speed limit? Can it be that concern for the lives and rights of others will affect the velocity at which you travel? Can it be that a man who chooses to be truly human—warmly compassionate, sensitive to others—will drive with as much concern for others as for himself?

Or does that sound like a little much? That's what Christ's recommendation to love your neighbor as yourself sounds like in the language of the road. It's difficult, of course. It's really possible only to the man who commits himself to take that first step: to love the Lord God with heart, soul, strength and mind.

It has a way of changing a man from the inside out. All the way out to his driving habits.

As you decide. There are three essentials to good driving: skill, knowledge and attitude; and the greatest of these is attitude.

In safe driving, it's the attitude that matters. And it had better matter a great deal to every one of us. "The average driver in the United States spends two hours a day behind the wheel of a car," reports the *Journal of the Society of Automotive Engineers.* There are 100 million cars on American roads, one for every two Americans. Since Henry Ford introduced the horseless carriage, about two million people have been killed on our nation's highways.

That's half a million more than all Americans killed in all our wars fought since the Boston Tea Party and the Battle of Bunker Hill.

"The death of one person is a tragedy; the death of a million people is a statistic."

Those words by Joseph Stalin reveal more than his attitude; they mirror our own unconcern over the fifty thousand traffic deaths a year.

Yes, some of them are caused by unsafe autos, but not a large percentage. Of course "death trap" intersections and "murder lane" roads are responsible for some—but not the major sector. The problem is people. Drivers are the dilemma. The National Safety Council reports that improper driving caused nearly 85 percent of all fatalities and 90 percent of all accidents last year.

The problem is attitudes.

Actually, after you talk about every problem, every cause, every factor in accidents, you are right back to the attitude of the man behind the wheel.

Why is the attitude paramount? Because in driving, most of our actions are by reflex, by instinct. It's our attitude at the time, and not our mind, that makes most of the instant decisions.

For example, according to engineer F. Bauer (Ford Motor Co.), on a crowded expressway, a driver:

> meets ten or more traffic events per second
> makes two or more conscious observations a second
> makes a decision every five seconds and performs 30
>   to 120 actions each minute.

Small wonder that studies by the Hughs Aircraft Company indicate that the U. S. motorist is under greater tension—as indicated by pulse, breathing, temperature—than an astronaut orbiting the earth.

What are the attitudes that count?

Concern for others, instead of selfishness and self-centered thinking.

Acceptance and forgiveness, in place of anger and irritable touchiness.

Caution and responsibility instead of thoughtlessness and carelessness.

Love, not indifference.

Such attitudes cannot be brought about by safety legislation, although there is one law that might do a great deal if it were followed: The law of God, contained in the Ten Commandments (see Ex 20:3-17). May I rephrase them for you, as they apply to drivers and driving?

> 1. Thou shalt have no other thought upon thy mind—when behind the wheel—except thy driving.
> 2. Thou shalt not make unto thee a god of thy horse-

power or worship thy clever driving or show off thy skill.

3. Thou shalt not take the laws of the road in vain, for the court will not hold him guiltless that breaketh the law.
4. Remember the rights of others, to respect them wholly.
5. Honor thy passengers and thy neighbor's passengers, that their days may be long upon the earth.
6. Thou shalt not kill.
7. Thou shalt not adulterate thy mind with alcohol, thy emotions with anger, thy attitudes with carelessness.
8. Thou shalt not steal—neither thy neighbor's eyes with thy headlights, nor his ear with thy horn, nor his passing with roadhogging, nor his scenery with thy litter.
9. Thou shalt not bear false witness with thy signals or lack of signal.
10. Thou shalt not covet thy neighbor's right-of-way.

But there is a greater law, a superior rule of life that gives the high rule for life at any speed. It is found in the teachings of Jesus Christ.

Christ's insistence that wrong attitudes are the basic problem rather than wrong actions is echoed by every traffic authority. Our police are preaching that anger, pride, selfishness, indifference, carelessness and negligence are turning our highways into a no-man's-land of wanton slaughter.

Christ showed us how to live above these in daily life. Those same principles can teach us to drive above them too. Christ remakes men by bringing new life, love and purpose to birth within them through the power of the Spirit.

"If we live in the Spirit, let us also [drive] in the Spirit"
(Gal 5:25).

"The Spirit which God gave us was . . . a spirit of power,
love, and self-control" (2 Ti 1:7, 20th Century N.T.).

Peter once wrote,

> See that your faith carries with it real goodness of life.
> Your goodness must be accompanied by knowledge, your
> knowledge by self-control, your self-control by . . .
> brotherliness, and your brotherliness must lead on to
> Christian love (2 Pe 1:5, 7, Phillips).

Love your neighbor as you love yourself (Mt 22:39),
whether he has Alberta plates or an Alabama number.

Every car you meet or pass is a neighbor you should
love.

Drive carefully—the life you save may be your neighbor's.

10

What's That You're Worrying About?

Scene one. You have every reason to be worried—your wife out walking a city street at night. She's only got a block to walk from the parking lot to the hotel where her meeting is held. But one block. Two alleyways to pass. Five hundred feet between street lights. A thug could be lurking, waiting for the click of a lady's heels. Then a quick hand over her mouth from behind, an arm around her waist knocking out all her wind, and she disappears into the alley.

Whew! You sit back in your chair trying to breathe a little easier and erase the worries from your mind. "Been watching too many of those crummy late crime movies," you grunt to yourself.

But it doesn't help. Sure you're worried about her, in the world we live in today. And you can't let this go on and on.

So what can you do? Play bodyguard? Impossible! Your schedule's too tight to even take care of yourself. Buy her some karate lessons? Her? With those little hands?

Then you know just the ticket. That little chrome .32 caliber purse gun that you saw in the window just a block uptown from your office. That could make the difference if she'd be willing to use it. And you could train her—after all, it'd be only close range.

Yeah, but she's no Annie Oakley. So what'll you do? Buy her the gun and surprise her? Try to prepare her by talking scare-talk for a week or two? Forbid her going out alone after dark, unless she carries it along?

Alternatives. What shall you do about giving your wife a bit of help in self-defense?

Enroll her in a karate course? No, she's too much woman, delicate hands, petite figure. Karate's not for her. What good would that do her if the guy is big, mean and armed? And besides, you don't want her getting that close to an attacker!

All right, why not a gun? She's good with her hands. She'd soon get the hang of handling it. And it's safe enough if she takes good care. No thug could expect her to draw a gun when he attacks. She'd have all the advantage of surprise.

But then, drawing a gun may force him to use his. Or lead him to even greater violence trying to seize it or stop her from using it. And if she did need to put it into action, would she? If she did, would you want her to live with the memory of shooting a man, even if she only wounded him?

No, maybe you ought to just get her one of those little tear gas bombs. But that may be as hard on her as on him unless she's fast and accurate in giving him the spray.

Or should you just pull back and quit letting her go any

place you're not sure about? But where could she go? No, you can't try that. You'd lose her either way.

How do you make this sort of decision? Just on the basis of what may be the safest for your wife? Then you'll not try any extra violence. Violence only breeds more violence. Or do you strike a compromise? A bit of protection, a little tear gas, and hope she comes out on top?

Whatever you choose, it's certain you try staying out of danger's path as responsibly as you both can. And where you can't, could you trust God to take care of the rest? That is a serious proposal, proven in life and practiced by many. Trusting God draws the fear out of life. After all, the only known antidote to fear is faith. And faith in Jesus Christ is the greatest basis for faith and the greatest resource for life and decision-making.

Scene two. You look at your little boy, and you've got to admit the fear's always there, even while your heart is lilting with his laughter. The fear for his future. What will he face? Go to school with a bunch of these delinquents and pre-dropouts? Be forced into a teen gang with no morals and a craze for dope, pot and secret sex orgies? Will you ever get a call at 2 A.M. saying, "This is the police department. If you will come down to sign bail for your son, we'll release him into your custody"?

Or will you see him leaving for war to some unknown corner of the world, to get shot up because some politicians are too bullish to cross this *t* or dot that *i* in some paper treaty?

Or will war reach you here, long before that, down the streets of your city? And violence sweeping everything before it. What could happen to your little man then?

You pick him up and let his burbling laughter bubble over you, but the fear is still there.

Then you wonder, *Why do I worry like this? Or does every father go through the same thing? And what can I do about it all, anyway?*

Alternatives. Why *shouldn't* you worry about your family's future? About the world your little boy will grow up in? Maybe you should just try looking on the brighter side. Build a little optimism into yourself and the boy. Overlook the problems. Of course, that won't shoo them away. Or shall you let it keep on bugging you, with the sort of fear that cramps the enjoyment of life? No, that sort of worry won't do anything for you, the boy or anyone else!

But how can you keep from it? Just avoid thinking over what might happen? You might, but there are news items wherever you look that remind you of which way our world seems to be going. And it sure isn't turning into a coast-to-coast PTA picnic.

Maybe the best thing is just bring your boy up to be a rough-tough master of all the arts of self-defense. Teach him to handle himself in any situation! Except, training in the skills of fighting and violence may just tend to get him into that much more of it.

Or should you try to escape it all? You can't just cry, "Stop the world! I want to get off," but you might find some safer habitat for your family. Move to better suburbia. Or out into the country. But really, where could you go to escape? There's no place to hide from the real dangers that threaten us.

These moves may be all right, but they just don't go far enough. Maybe the best you can do is build the kind of strength and character into that little son that will stand by him no matter what he faces? If he's been taught, or if he's caught the kind of inner principle that builds stability even in the midst of turmoil, that could make the difference. That's faith. The faith in God that can give a man a style of life worth teaching his son. And a strength for living even in very difficult times.

As you decide. In East Germany, I was talking with a lady in her forties. "Yes, we have no children," she told me. "It is such a pity." Then looking first over both shoulders, she continued, "But here behind the iron curtain, it is a comfort to be childless. Oh, my husband and I are lonely, yes. Children are so beautiful when they are small, but here there is no future for them."

The place? A restaurant in Wittenburg, Martin Luther's hometown. We sat talking by the street where the great Reformer had walked to nail his Ninety-five Theses of religious liberty on the church door.

But now, seventy miles away, the Iron Curtain. And here, no future.

Before you heave a sigh of relief because you live in a "free country," wait. Think.

What about your children?

Do they have a future? Do they?

"I will never be a father," a college man told me. "I want no part in bringing children into a world with no future."

And a young father told me, "Every time I sit and watch my kiddies play, I worry. I wonder what future is there for them—will the world last long enough? Will they live to see the day when they will sit and watch their children?"

I must confess, I wonder. I fight worry, too. Will my

little daughters ever manage to grow up to real woman-
hood in a world where a thirteen-year-old virgin is a
laughingstock? Where honesty is for the squares? Integrity for fools only?

Will they someday live under a totalitarian state? Will
they have to learn to live like moles in bomb shelters? Will
they become garbage pickers in the radioactive ruins of our
civilization—if they survive its sterilizing blast?

But let's not pretend we are the only ones who care.
If you care about the future of your family, know this:
God cares, infinitely more than both of us.

You don't have to carry all your personal cares on your
own shoulders. Why should you live as if all of your life
and future depends on your own ability to maneuver or
manipulate circumstances?

God cares about you. Enough to work things in your
life to make a difference.

The Bible says, "Let Him have all your worries and
cares, for He is always thinking about you and watching
everything that concerns you" (1 Pe 5:7; Living Letters).
Phillips states it this way: "You can throw the whole
weight of your anxieties upon him, for you are his personal
concern."

"I stopped trying to be God," a fellow Christian told me
today.

"When?" I asked with a smile, but I knew just what he
meant. Since God cares about you, why should you burden
yourself with a God-size load of worries that belong to
Him?

When the outward look terrifies me and I begin to fear,
I look to God. I love God. I feel His answering tug of love

on my heart. And I look around for the fears for the future
—my future, my children's future—but they are gone.

I just believe I can leave tomorrow in God's hands. Certainly God will be there tomorrow. We'll face tomorrow
together! After all, that's what Jesus said. "Don't worry
at all then about tomorrow. . . . One day's trouble is enough
for one day. Your Heavenly Father knows. . . . Set your
heart on . . . his goodness (Mt 6:34, 32-33, Phillips).

"Last night my little son and I were working in the
shop," a carpenter friend of mine told me. "I watched my
boy at work, imagining him as a grown man. Suddenly I
saw him twenty years from now, in a different world. It
looked like a military state. There were hard times, ter-
rific pressures.

"What should I do?" the carpenter asked. "How do I
prepare him for anything the future holds?"

"Love the boy," I answered. "And teach him to love.
Teach him to love others. To love God. To love God more
than anything. More than money, pleasure or a successful
career. And meanwhile, let him see it in your own life.
If he walks through the future with God, he'll be all right.
Won't he?"

"Why, yes," said the carpenter, tension draining from
his face. "Why, yes, he can walk into *any* future with
God."

11

You Can Quit Anytime?

Scene one. So you're working down at the shop, and the guy on the machine next to you, who has a habit of talking twenty-four hours a day (except for when he's lighting up another cigarette), runs out of smokes. And then the hollering starts.

"Hey, any of you guys got a smoke? Aw, c'mon, Bill, don't shake your head like that. Hey, Nick, how about a cig? For the love of Mike, you quit too? What'sa matter with you guys? You got the cancer panic?

"What do you know about that? So they quit, huh? If those two can kick the habit, then, phooey, I'll give them a week. They'll be lucky to make it through the day.

"Yeah, well, I'm laughin' but it's not such a bad idea, you know? So I'd live a lot longer. Maybe it's just without the cigarettes you think it's a lot longer?

"Not that I'm in any hurry to read my name in the obits. I can see it now: 'Joe Black deceased. Committed suicide with a cigarette lighter.' Don't sound like much, does it? How do I explain that to my Maker? I only got one life. I do sort of hate to see it go up in smoke."

And he goes on talking at you and arguing with himself while he runs his lathe by the skill of habit. And you tune him out, as usual. But this time, he's set you thinking. The guy's hit on more truth than he knows. You do sort of hate to see your life go up in smoke. Sure, you're tired of having him bumming all your cigarettes day in, day out. And even more tired of that chronic cough of yours.

So what shall you do about the cigarettes? Give them the flip and go through life with an empty face? Or forget the cancer scare and enjoy them?

Alternatives. Well, now that you're at a moment of serious thought, it won't hurt to explore it. So you're sure that smoke isn't doing your lungs any good. Not that your cough is serious. It's just a little persistent. Occasionally raw. But you've plenty of time to see a doctor. He'd only tell you to quit. You already know that would be good. So why pay for advice you don't need?

Maybe you should forget it all and keep on lighting up? Sure, it may chop off a few years of your life. But that's all! Cancer? No, not you. You've never had a sick day in your life. Heart disease? Well, there's a little of that running in the family, but no more than in anybody else's.

So that's the way the logic bounces.

Unless. Unless you try looking at both sides of the cigarette pack. There may be another side for you to consider before you make up your mind.

Each day 822 persons die from causes associated with smoking. More than one every two minutes. Do you want to go that badly?

Maybe a talk with your doctor would be worth it after all?

Or maybe you've got the guts it takes to unhook and go

free? Not by tapering off. That seldom works for anyone. It takes a clean break.

It could give you a whole new clean feeling, a feeling of health. And maybe peace. After all, it does matter what you do with your life, doesn't it? God gave you only one life to live. Why let it all go up in smoke? Why not discover how He meant for it to be lived? With His style of life. And with His strength.

Scene two. So it's your first week at the new office job, and you've gone out to lunch with three of the guys who seem to be on the inside of everything around the place. They're filling you in and you're doing your best to look in-the-know on it all when the waitress finally comes for your orders.

"Cocktails all around?" she asks. "Make mine Scotch and water," the guy nearest says. "Same for me," the next says. "You too?" she says to the fellow across from you. "Oh, no, strictly a bourbon man," he says. Then she turns expectantly to you. "What's yours?" she asks.

Strange how many thoughts can zip by in a split second, when suddenly you're in a spot you didn't anticipate, you don't relish, and you hardly know how to escape.

Shall you order and fit right in with the guys or keep that resolution you made three years ago when you came home sloshed once too often from a party and had that horrible blowup with your wife. That was when you came to your own moment of truth.

"Look at you," she had said. "You're turning into a regular Saturday night lush." That's when it hit you. The little woman was right. You were on the sauce too often, and your job, family, your whole life were suffering.

Was that what made you swear off? Or was it the acci-

dent you almost had on the way home a week later? Or
the memory of your favorite uncle who leaned on the stuff
so hard that he wiped out at forty-five?

Whatever went into that decision, you decided to knock
it off. Permanently. And you did. It hadn't been easy,
but you stayed off the stuff. Till now. And here you are
with a waitress waiting, pencil to pad, "What's yours?"
still on her lips.

So what's one little drink to get to know the guys? So
what? You can always cool it later. Or should you make
it coffee and let them think what they like?

Alternatives. Well, you could go along for one round.
Show the guys that you're one of the crowd. Later you can
knock off again. Of course, what makes you think it'll be
easier to order a coke the next time than this?

Or you could decide that this new set of business asso-
ciates demand a few new ideas. Sure you'll still stay off
the social drinks where one drink soon gets to a couple
refills, another splash or two, then a couple "while your
ups," and soon you're feeling no pain. Yeah. But maybe
you could handle a few business drinks again and stay off
the rest. If a liquid lunch is in order—then order it. So
what will it hurt?

Or do you have to admit that for you drinking is drinking? And bending an elbow at lunch will soon mean tip-
ping a few at dinner, and from then on. Is it possible that
you—your wife—your kids—your future—are all going to
be happier without fogging your brain and fueling your
system with you-know-what?

And speaking of your kids, it'd be rough to have them
remember you with the same tone of voice you use to
describe dear old hundred-proof Uncle Bill. (God rest his

soul.) And if someday they start on the same drinking routine, what'll you have to say?

So what if you do order a coke? Who says you'll lose the guys' respect? You may gain it all fast. Who says you've got to follow suit to be accepted? They may be glad to have you drive them back to the office.

And look what you gain. You keep faith with your wife. Keep your kids' respect. You feel right. You're a more responsible man—in any situation. You're a step nearer becoming the kind of man God intended you to be. Clean, wholesome, decisive and at peace with yourself. With all that, who needs a drink?

Scene three. You're somewhere in that foggy state that blankets you when you're lying half awake waiting for the alarm to do its thing. You kick your feet out on the floor, unglue your eyelids with a forefinger, and mumble to yourself as you try to shut the pesky clock off.

"Oh, wow, my head," you grumble aloud. "How'd I get home? Last thing I remember was passing out at that party."

You head for the shower to shock yourself awake. "Boy, if I could just shower the fog off my brain. Why'd I go and get juiced up again?" That's when your conscience needles you with a good question: "Why don't you quit?"

"Look, who are you, wise mouth?"

("I'm just your better sense, and it's been a mighty long time since you've even listened to me, let alone used me.")

"All right, so I'm all wet."

("You're hardly dry.")

"So I'm an old soak with a botched-up life. But what can I do about it? Just live with it. And the only way I can do that is gloss over the mess with a few drinks."

You shut off the shower and try to switch off your conscience. But with limited success.

It's getting harder and harder to live without props. And you've gotten into leaning more and more on the quick release you get from a few drinks. But inside you're fighting yourself, fighting the world.

But what can you do about it? Give up drinking? Be easier to give up thinking. You've got to admit that it's grown to be a pretty big part of your life.

Alternatives. You can accept drinking as one of life's necessities and try to set up a few ground rules that will help keep it in control, like no drinking before six, never drink alone, refuse all liquid lunches or limit yourself strictly to one. But maybe it's already gone too far?

Perhaps it boils down to only one set of alternatives for you: Either you go on loading up and turning off with your favorite brand, or you turn it off. All the way off. Once for all.

But going dry is no cinch. Alcoholics Anonymous can offer a great deal of help. If you're willing to accept the name and submit yourself to their disciplines. Your doctor may offer specific help if you've some problem uniquely your own. Or there are all sorts of self-help plans supposed to stiffen your spine or straighten out that elbow that tends to bend so easily. These may be of help.

However you try, or wherever you turn for help, one thing you'll need: strength of will inside yourself, and a new strength to draw on from outside yourself.

As A.A. suggests, you'll need to get to know God.

Yes, God can provide the sort of outside help that goes to work inside where you need it. In fact, some men discover that He is the greatest source of strength for beginning a new life or for shedding that old one that just doesn't want to go.

As you decide. When you think of taking that next cigarette or drink, ask yourself if there is any difference if a man commits suicide fast or slow. Isn't a man just as responsible for a gradual death by delinquent abuse of his body as for a quick deliberate death by his own hand?

Will not the Creator ask, "What have you done with the life I gave you to live?"

Does not the sixth commandment, "Thou shalt not kill" (Ex 20:13), apply to a cigarette lighter and the cocktail shaker as well as knife or gun?

But even if you should be too tough for cancer to catch, too hearty for heart disease to fell, are there not other reasons why you should quit smoking?

Economically, smoking's a sure way to turn a major part of yourself—your time, and your life turned into the negotiable form called money—into noxious ashes. A lifetime of smoking would purchase a home, a college education, a round-the-world tour or many useful acts of service.

Socially, it utterly disregards Christ's command to love your neighbor as yourself. Not just the offensive practice of fouling up everybody else's right to free, clean air; not just in forcing smoke and its harmful effects on others who detest it; not just in drenching trains, planes, restaurants everywhere with the stale, sour odor, the murky smog, the ashes, butts, and fire hazards, but also in the pressure that your smoking places automatically on the young, the impressionable, the quick-to-conform people who snap up what others are doing, hoping to find a buttress for their insecurities.

And there's the personal way you identify yourself as a

user, burning up your health, your wholeness, your clean wholesomeness of personhood and personality.

Which leads to the greatest reason for rejecting cigarettes. God wants your friendship. It is His greatest wish. He proved that by the length He went to show us His forgiving love. Calvary, the cross—remember?

He wants to live life with you. "Move over," He says. "Don't try to occupy your whole life. You can't. You were made to share it with Me. Let Me go it with you." The Bible says,

> Have you forgotten that your body is the temple of the Holy Spirit, who lives in you, and is God's gift to you, and that you are not the owner of your own body? You have been bought, and at what a price! Therefore bring glory to God in your body (1 Co 6:19-20, Phillips).

That calls for all of your life gladly, wholly lived to its fullest, highest best.

Life is so short, even at its best. Then why not live it cleanly, completely for God. With only one life to live, why let it go up in smoke?

And about that next drink. You *can* quit drinking, even though the habit dies hard and slowly.

Many people never rid themselves, because they make a feeble attempt; or they fail because they didn't arm themselves with the intestinal fortitude, the emotional will to win, or the simple knowledge of how to go about it.

William James, the great Harvard psychologist of the last generation, gave four fundamental steps to breaking any habit. They are principles that apply to any change, but are especially appropriate to your battle with drinking.

1. Start yourself off on the new way of life with as much momentum, resolution and insulation as possible.

2. Don't permit yourself to make a single exception to your new rule until the new way of life is firmly implanted (and that will be a long time).

3. Once you have determined to break the habit, do it at the first opportune, appropriate, advantageous moment.

4. Don't just give up the habit and then meekly idle along without it, passively bearing the discomforts of life without your old crutch. Fight these temporary difficulties by replacing them with meaningful, worthwhile substitutes. Find ways of exercising your convictions and your new commitments.

To this, add a fifth step, a universal one: Laugh. Use your sense of humor. Don't take the crisis of breaking an old habit too seriously or tragically. Don't allow yourself to steep in self-pity. Turn off the sweet sympathy and the martyr feelings.

Laugh at the nuisance, the burden, the problem that the old habit once was to you.

Laughter is liberating. Use it.

Now, where shall you begin?

1. Know yourself. Understand your reasons for drinking; examine them carefully and see them for what they are.

2. Decide to stop abruptly, completely and permanently. No tapering off. No cheating on the side. Cut it off cleanly, totally and finally.

3. Fortify your resolution sufficiently to withstand all urges and urging to drink. The greater your buildup of determination, the more certain your victory.

4. Burn all bridges behind you. Tell your friends that

you're through with drinking. Tell them why. Tell them that it's only a part of a sweeping change of opening your life totally to God. If they're friends, they'll respect and support you.

5. Utilize any and all opportunities for assistance. Get involved with others who have found new life in Jesus Christ. Talk it over honestly, candidly. Such friendships are a great source of strength.

6. Adopt substitutes for your old habitual actions. Emphasize more outdoor life, recreation and relaxation in a more healthful way. Begin pursuing those hobbies, service opportunities, friendships, activities that you've wished you had time for.

Substitute helpful, healthful things for the old "signal drinking." Tea before dinner, bouillon before lunch, or whatever alternatives fit your taste.

Instead of a nightcap, try a walk or a hot tub followed by a cold shower. It will relax you more and go a long way toward relieving tensions.

Plan your schedule in advance. Fill it full of things you'll enjoy. Invest your time in others. Avoid leaving blocks of unplanned idle time to tempt you toward drinking again.

7. Confirm your convictions by deliberately emphasizing the advantages of nondrinking. Recognize the points of improvement brought by quitting the habit. Remind yourself of the difference your change has made. Not primarily the difference from others, but the difference from what you were and the difference from what you would be if you were still on the bottle.

8. Help others to free themselves. As you discover all the advantages, share them. Nothing strengthens your

resolution to stand by the decision like getting involved in assisting people with deeper problems than your own.

9. Pray. Don't try to go it alone. Why should you? God offers the help to set you free. Why not accept it? And the friendship of another person who has kicked the habit or who can understand exactly what you face can be of immeasurable help.

Make the decision for good; but don't try to fight the whole battle at once. Live a day at a time. One day's victory is good enough for one day.

Pray: "God, supply Your strength for my weakness. Make me adequate to live this day without any crutch. Give me the courage to become the clean, wholesome man You intended me to be."

Pray whenever you need the strength. You'll discover how close God really is. All the time.

There's a whole wealth of exciting discoveries ahead of you in this life with God.

Quitting drinking is only a step toward a new, clean life. But it's a step. It's the step you should take now.

12

Care Enough to Communicate?

Scene one. So the wife of this guy where you work died four days ago. Man, you feel for him, but you sure don't relish going to see him. What on earth do you say? But you can't ignore him. So what do you do? Then you hear he's in the office this morning just to check his mail. You can't avoid it any longer. You go down to talk. It's obvious he's glad you stopped by. You see, it turns out you're the only guy in the office who cared enough to come talk. And once he starts telling you about it all, it's kind of like the dam breaks, and he lets the bitterness about it all sorta bleed out.

He says, "I can't figure it out—why her? Why did my wife have to die? Why? I go home at night and the kids are waiting, looking lost. If religion means anything at all, why did my wife die? This tears me up. I don't get it. The kids miss her like crazy. So do I. You'd think religion would help give me some answers—but it hasn't! I don't feel anything—I'm just numb.

So what do you tell a man with a broken heart? What can you say? When his world's caved in and nothing makes sense to him. What do you say? "Keep a stiff upper lip"; "Every cloud has a silver lining"; "Look on the brighter side"; "It could have been worse"; or any of the other things you've heard people parrot? Hardly! What shall you do? Edge away and escape as soon as you can?

Alternatives. Well, you can get off the spot by saying the conventional things in a solemn tone of voice. Give your sympathy and all that. And when the conversation lags, excuse yourself with a medium handshake.

Or you can mentally kick yourself for getting caught with one of these fellows in trouble who needs somebody to lean on. *If I get out of this one,* you vow silently, *I'll steer clear in the future.*

Or you could shed all your cool, protective layers and really feel for the guy. Let it really grab you. Who says a man has to be tough-skinned and hardhearted? To be really human, you don't just skid over life's surface. You feel others' joy and pain by caring.

Or maybe you've already learned that by going through tragedy yourself? If so, you'll do what really counts. You'll listen. He isn't interested in a speech from you anyway. If anything will count with him now, it's just the fact that you care. Care enough to listen. An understanding, listening ear may be the greatest gift you can give him.

Or you could offer him the only other encouragement there is. Faith. Not that Christian faith will explain in acceptable, logical terms why his wife died. Suffering and dying are all part of this tragic world. But it can give him the assurance that God is deeply involved in his tragedy. Caring, and sharing the load. He can know that God went through this same thing when His Son got involved in human sorrows and troubles and got killed for His interest.

That's how God knows firsthand. And cares enough to stay close to a man with His extra strength and peace.

Scene two. You're inching along in the rush hour traffic, a little impatient to get home. You're pushing the buttons on your car radio to get to the music you tolerate best, when "News at Thirty" catches you.

The announcer runs past an airplane hijacking, a murder in the ghetto, a mugging in the park, some stuff about the stock market. Then tagged on to the end, this note: "An accident took the life of a young suburban housewife at 3:17 this afternoon. A semitrailer went out of control at the intersection of Vine and McFaddon, crushing the late model white convertible—"

That's all you hear. Suddenly you know it's your wife. She said last evening that she had an appointment at the hairdresser's over on Vine Street. And that's her car—a white, late model convertible—and the right time—she'd have been turning off onto McFadden to pick up the kids when they got out of school at 3:30.

You clutch the steering wheel till your knuckles cramp, cursing the slow traffic that holds you back. There ahead— a service station. You signal frantically to the guy on your right. He finally sees you and lets you pull through. You dash to the phone booth, feed in a dime, and dial your home phone. There—it rings once, twice.

Suddenly out of nowhere a million memories rise. Tender memories of times when you should have told her better how much you care. Painful memories of senseless differences that arose between you and you were too pigheaded to put them down. Guilty memories of the deep hurts that still lie quietly buried in your relationship. "Why couldn't we accept each other?" you ask yourself. "Why couldn't we be genuine and live honestly?"

It rings a third time.

And then her voice saying, "Hello."

"Hi, darling," you say, a rush of emotion coloring your tone.

"Oh, hi," she says, "what's the matter?"

"Oh, nothing, nothing at all," you lie in reply. "Just wanted to tell you—I'll be a few minutes late."

You hang up, and slip in behind the wheel of your car; but you sit there wondering. Should you sit down and talk it out with your wife? Should you let this incident tear your heart enough to tell her how much you really care and accept her? Could you build the kind of intimacy that a moment ago you were wishing you had? What shall you do about your relationship with your wife, now that you've seen it as it really is?

Alternatives. Should you forget it? Write it off as an accident scare and go on just as you are? You've been surviving it; why try for anything more?

Strange how an accident, a threat of death, or some other tragedy can bring you to an instant moment of truth, isn't it?

You could decide to do something, like telling her how you felt this afternoon when you were sure she'd been involved in an accident; tell her about the second thoughts you had. Then try to persuade her to talk it out, together.

It could be that she's had the same sort of ideas at some time or other. And you might be on the same wavelength right away.

Maybe you should keep mum about it all, but just be the kind of mate you wish you were. Just be more accepting, more understanding, just show her you care. Actions out-speak words anyway.

Or are the reservations in your marriage so deep that you need help? Have the old patterns set so firmly that only an outside person—like a marriage counselor or a pastor—could open things between you?

Or should you take it just as seriously as you did when you thought it was too late, when you were sure that the accident on the news involved her? If you did, you could live life on a new level—with openness and acceptance between the two of you. A new faith in each other, maybe even a new love. That could make your whole life different.

As you decide. The art of truly communicating with others—in marriage, or just in friendships—is the art of living richly, deeply and with meaning. That calls for more than superficial interest in others. It demands caring. Caring enough to love. Caring enough to be understanding. Caring enough to listen to the other person. In normal daily friendships, listening is the first requirement of love.

Do you know how to listen? Or do your eyes stray and betray your wandering interests? (A good listener listens with his eyes too, you know.)

Do you let others' words and ideas fly by while you plan your next comment, cooking up some sage word with which to stun them at the first opportunity?

Do you interrupt others or, even worse, second-guess them, trying to finish the line for a friend, or coach him when he stumbles for a word?

Do you probe, question, interrogate, cross-examine, suggesting impatience or superiority?

Or can you truly listen? Can you go beyond merely

hearing words and phrases to catch the ideas? And beyond the ideas, to the feelings? Beyond the expressions to the true intent?

That's listening. With love for others.

Love is a warm listener!

Haven't you experienced it? Have you ever talked with someone who listened with such abandon and attention to what you were trying to say that it drew you out? Called forth your best. Even helped clarify your thoughts by the very quality of his listening.

Or have you started out to vent your inner agonies and complain bitterly against your circumstances, but your friend's understanding love given in complete attention made you see things in a new light and instead of collecting a quart of sweet sympathy, you simply unloaded your problem?

That's the power of listening love.

And when you discover that a friend is going through tragedy, you show whether you really care by how you listen.

If you were ever involved in a personal tragedy, did you want someone to talk to you? Did you need a speech of sympathy? Or a little sermonette of encouragement?

No, no! You wanted someone who loved you enough to sit down and listen to your feelings, to give understanding and acceptance in spite of your problem. Right?

And the people who didn't care enough to listen hurt you deeply. No matter all the nice-nice things they said or how well they kept up the running patter of sweet nothings. If they gave you the standard treatment, a flawlessly worded, lovely, little speech, the farther it went, the more distant it became. You wanted to shake them and say: "Come back. I don't want your beautiful bouquets of words. I want *you*." Who needs an eloquent cluster of phrases? We want the bread of human understanding. No matter how polished, perfect and multifaceted the gems of truth, they offer no nourishment. You can't eat diamonds. Even if they are "forever."

Love is listening. Caring is hearing.

Love is the opening of your life to another.

Through sincere interest, simple attention, sensitive listening, compassionate understanding and honest sharing.

An open ear is the only believable sign of an open heart. You learn to understand life—you learn to live—as you learn to listen.

To love your neighbor is to listen to him as you listen to yourself. The golden rule of friendship—to listen to others as you would have them listen to you.

Listening—it's the first key to true friendship, loyalty and understanding between any and all persons in all relationships: parent-child, husband-wife, employer-employee, friend and friend.

Now about that deeper communication between husband and wife that demands even more self-giving, even more of love.

When husband and wife talk together, their conversation runs on a minimum of two levels: the visible, verbal level of words, gestures, expressions, and the invisible, nonverbal level of attitudes and feelings. The second is the most important but it is only possible when the first level is happening.

To illustrate: When a singer sings correctly, his voice is pleasantly clear and in tune. But it also sets off ringing overtones of resonance which are the true beauty of his sound. The overtones are the beautiful part, but they only exist when the voice tones are being made.

In identical fashion, the overtones of silent empathy, of nonverbal understanding, only exist when our spoken words provide a genuine relation and a true revelation of ourselves and our love. The perfect description of this is found in the Bible:

> If your experience of Christ's encouragement and love means anything to you, if you have known . . . all that it means in kindness and deep sympathy, . . . live together in harmony, live together in love, as though you had only one mind and one spirit between you. Never act from motives of rivalry or personal vanity, but in humility think more of [each other] than you do of yourselves. None of you should think only of his own affairs, but each should learn to see things from [others'] . . . point of view (Phil 2:1-4, Phillips).

Such love moves from revelation of self to participation in the other person. Each person truly revealing himself to the other thus participates in the other's life.

This is obviously done by giving the present of a listening ear of love, of hearing what the other person actually felt and said, not what we thought they said.

But in a deeper sense, it is done by giving your presence. By really being with, and by truly being present, when you are with the other person. This is attentiveness. The deep attention of love. If it has seldom been experienced, it may seem almost threatening. As it was to the wife whose husband dropped his paper and turned full attention to her. She snapped, annoyed anew, "Now you're deliberately listening just to confuse me."

True communication between husband and wife is mutual participation in feelings and frustrations; in insight and understandings; in disappointments and depression; or in excitement and happiness. Each participates in the other's experiences. Communication is born in communion, the common-union of lives.

The Bible sums it all up:

> Accept life, and be most patient and tolerant with one another, always ready to forgive if you have a difference. . . . Forgive as freely as the Lord has forgiven you. And, above everything else, be truly loving, for love is the golden chain of all the virtues (Col 3:12-13, Phillips).

Can you truly communicate? Yes, yes, you can.

If you are willing to open your life in revelation, in self-disclosure, in the openness of selfless love.

And if you are willing to give yourself in participation, in selfless attention, understanding and empathy.

That is the way Christ can build your lives together into maturity and bind your marriage together into true unity. Through open, mutual communication—communion and union. Through love.